COLLECTOR'S ENCYCLOPEDIA
of
Roseville
POTTERY

VOLUME 1
REVISED EDITION

SHARON & BOB HUXFORD
and
MIKE NICKEL

COLLECTOR BOOKS

A Division of Schroeder Publishing Co., Inc.

Roseville Display Sign, 1940s, 5" x 8", $3,000.00 – 3,500.00.

The current values of this book should be used only as a guide. They are not intended to set prices, which can vary from one section of the country to another. Auction prices as well as dealer prices vary and are affected by condition as well as demand. Neither the authors nor the publisher assumes any responsibility for any losses that might be incurred as a result of consulting this guide.

On the front cover:
Della Robbia floor vase, 22", eight-color, slip decorated, full signature of Helen Smith, NPA.
Only one known. *Photo by David Rago Galleries.*
On the back cover:
Hollywood Ware vase, bears label (see mark #2, page 20), 6", $600.00 – 700.00.
From the collection of Bill Barnett and Terry Moore.

Cover design by Beth Summers
Book design by Karen Smith

Searching for a Publisher?

We are always looking for people knowledgeable within their fields. If you feel that there is a real need for a book on your collectible subject and have a large comprehensive collection, contact Collector Books.

Collector Books
P.O. Box 3009
Paducah, Kentucky 42002-3009

www.collectorbooks.com

Copyright © 2001 by Sharon and Bob Huxford

→ Contents ←

33½" Pine Cone jardiniere (#632-12",
impressed mark) and pedestal.
Blue, $7,000.00 – 8,000.00.
Brown, $4,500.00 – 5,000.00.
Green, $3,000.00 – 3,500.00.

→ Dedication ←

This book is dedicated to
Ed and Thelma, Marvin and Jan, and
Roseville collectors everywhere.

"The genius of the artist here calls together the primeval elements beneath his feet, to do his bidding. Earth, water, and fire bend to the task and to him bring the product of their united labors. He clothes the varied shapes of beauty in the soft rich colors that please him best. And then across each shining blossom he lays with exquisite grace a nodding iris…a spray of apple blossoms…or a rosy thistle bloom…And in their fadeless triumphant beauties sends them forth to adorn and bless the homes and lives of the children of men…."
Lura Milburn Cobb

→ About the Authors ←

Michael (Mike) Nickel is one of the country's best known authorities on Roseville Pottery. Since 1970 he has been not only an avid collector but also a dealer, specializing in the finest examples available. Many pieces from his collection are featured in Volume II. He has personally edited this edition, and we are happy to be able to offer our readers much more in-depth information than ever before, due entirely to his efforts. Shape numbers have been added wherever possible, the pricing structure in many instances has been broken down by color, corrections have been made to the text to reflect new information that has come to light since our earlier research, and values have been updated to more accurately represent current market activity.

Mike is a retired advertising creative director and is a former officer of the American Art Pottery Association, having the distinction of holding the Life Member Number One membership in that organization. He is married to Cynthia (Cindy) Horvath, and together they have written *Kay Finch Ceramics, Her Enchanted World*. They are full-time antiques dealers and travel the circuit extensively.

Mike Nickel • P.O. Box 456 • Portland, MI 48875
517-647-7646 • Buy, sell, appraise
e-mail: mandc@voyager.net

After writing their first book, *The Story of Fiesta*, published in 1974 (now in its 9th edition), the Huxfords became Pottery Editors for Collector Books and in that capacity wrote several other books on various Ohio potteries. The *Collector's Encyclopedia of Roseville Pottery* and the *Collector's Catalog of Early Roseville* were published in 1976; new releases in 1978 included the *Collector's Encyclopedia of McCoy Pottery,* the *Collector's Encyclopedia of Brush-McCoy Pottery,* and the *Collector's Catalog of Brush-McCoy*

Pottery. The *Collector's Encyclopedia of Weller Pottery* was published in 1979, and in 1980 they wrote the *Collector's Encyclopedia of Roseville Pottery, Volume II.* Since 1982 they have been editors of *Schroeder's Antiques Price Guide; Schroeder's Collectible Toys, Antique to Modern; Garage Sale & Flea Market Annual;* and *Wanted To Buy.*

Pine Cone floor vase, #912-15".
Blue, $4,000.00 – 4,500.00. Brown, $3,000.00 – 3,500.00.
Green, $2,000.00 – 2,500.00.

⇢ Acknowledgments ⇠

The following six paragraphs are from our original book, published in 1976. The help of these fine people needs to be acknowledged today with the same appreciation we felt more than 25 years ago.

❖ With deepest gratitude we wish to acknowledge the assistance of many, many wonderful people who have so generously contributed to this study.

Ed and Thelma Newman have been Roseville collectors for several years and have been our "right arm" over the past several months. At considerable expense, they have added many pieces of pottery to their already extensive collection, so that it would be available to us. Several hundred pieces of fine pottery from their collection were photographed for this book. To these dear friends… a special "Thank you."

We're also very grateful to our friends, Marvin and Jeanette Stofft. Their collection contains many fine examples of the Rozane lines of 1905 and 1906, and because we were so graciously allowed to photograph them as well as several other lines, nearly all of the Roseville lines have been well represented. We thank them for this opportunity and for the hours we spent with them discussing the pottery and learning from their experience.

Donald and Zeta Alexander have shown us very gracious hospitality on several occasions, and we want to thank them, not only for their encouragement, but also for allowing us to reproduce for our book their own compositions of the Roseville trademarks. Several pieces from their collection are shown in black and white in the picture section.

Buck and Marilyn Jones loaned us several beautiful color slides, which they allowed us to reproduce, for which we thank them very much. Their excellent photography was done by P. L. Hill, Tulsa, Oklahoma.

Other collectors, dealers, and friends who have supplied pottery, or helped in numerous other ways are Maxine Fergeson, Wayside Antiques, Zanesville, Ohio; Betty Blair, Catalpa Heights Antiques, Jackson, Ohio; Norm and Martha Miller, Schube's Antiques, Franklin, Indiana; Harry and Martha Rheapp; Larry, Linda, and Tony Newman; Virginia Buxton; Bob and Maxine Lang. Thanks to Dana Curtis, our very fine photographer…the pictures are just beautiful, Dana! And lastly, to the staff at the Ohio Historical Society, and especially to Arlene Peterson, Reference Librarian, we send our appreciation. ❖

We're very grateful to Bill Barnett and Terry Moore who provided us with some wonderful photographs of rarities from their collection — the Hollywood Ware on the back cover of this book as well as both pieces shown on the covers of Volume II.

⇢ Price Guide Information ⇠

The prices in this volume as well as in Volume II represent the high end of average retail. They are for items in mint condition, that is to say first-quality pieces with no incurred damage such as chips, hairlines, glaze flaking or staining. Certain factory flaws, such as glazed-over chips, pieces not truly molded, leaning or otherwise slightly irregular; poorly finished mold lines; faint embossing; poor color or careless decoration, may also decrease the value of a piece considerably. Crazing is that fine network of tiny lines caused by uneven expansion and contraction between body and glaze. You can expect to find it to some extent on items from any production period, and in moderate amounts it should not affect value. A properly restored item (with an invisible mend) may sell for 70% to 80% of mint value, depending on the extent of the restoration.

In earlier lines, the presence of a round Rozane seal (ceramic wafer) or the seal with the attached chevron containing the line name will add at least 25% to our values, possibly even more, especially on these lines: Mara, Mongol, and Crystalis. On the early handpainted lines, items with an artist's cipher command a 20% premium, particularly if that artist's work is highly regarded. Portraits of animals or people are worth much more than a simple floral design.

Measurements have been rounded off to the nearest half-inch. Shape numbers have been added whenever possible, and where warranted, pricing has been broken down by color. See the chapter Line Descriptions and Dates of Introduction to determine approximate dates and for information on color assortments. The chapter entitled Roseville's Trademarks will help pinpoint the time frames when the various marks were used.

The art of pottery…how and when it all began…is an uncertainty whose revelation is obstructed by countless eons and civilizations — obliterating from all but our imagination, glimpses of the ancient cultures. Perhaps women, needing pots for food and water, with an inventiveness born of necessity, noticed how the sun-baked ruts in the clay soil held the water long after a sudden summer shower had passed…or a loving father, who days before had fashioned from the pliable, yellow clay a crude horse to entertain his young child, stood and pondered over its brick-like texture.

In such a way, then, as civilizations and cultures progressed and as man aspired to continually improve and improvise…so the development of the ceramic art progressed. In the beginning, man shaped these crude vessels of clay by hand…perhaps learning to mold bowls around a smooth round rock or coiling thinly rolled strips to form the sides of cylindrical forms. He left them to harden and bake in the sun. Then, to the previously utilitarian clayware, he began to add embellishments and decorations, delighted with the opportunity to satisfy the innate desire man has always possessed, to express with his hands the beauty his senses have revealed to his soul.

As knowledge increased, crude kilns were constructed. Progressing further…by some stroke of genius, the potter's wheel was developed, one of man's first mechanical inventions…indicating the preeminence of this art in ancient cultures. Its invention was claimed by both the Chinese and the Egyptians.

Shards of ancient pottery, as well as clay tablets and the painted walls of the tombs, are remarkably preserved. Through their study, modern man has been provided with much understanding of these bygone civilizations.

Existing evidence indicates an almost simultaneous development in China and Egypt…Greek and Roman cultures merged…and as the Roman Empire widened with each new conquest, the science of ceramics pervaded the European countries.

The knowledge of pottery that passed on to France and Spain had reached a high degree of proficiency and sophistication. From these peoples, this knowledge advanced to Britain.

The ancient Chinese were responsible for spreading the art to Japan. The inventive Japanese artisans ornamented their pottery with designs in relief by pinching up the still damp clay…and adding still more design by incising lines in artistic arrangements.

Although evidence has been found of glazed pottery in ancient Egypt, and at a somewhat later period in Chinese history, nowhere else has ever been found the lustrous glazes of Persia. In this country, the ancient potters learned the use of metallic oxides to produce a glaze that could simulate the pattern of metal. After the Arabs conquered Persia, though they had no art of their own, they quickly absorbed the knowledge of the Persian artists. Through the Moors, who were also of the Islamic religion, the potters' art was carried on to Africa.

The sgraffito technique is known to have been used in Italy after the fall of the Roman Empire. Here was developed the first general use of the tin enamel called majolica. Italian workmen carried the art to France; thus the French were able to produce a ware almost identical. This French tin enameled pottery was called faience…so named after the city of Faenza, the great pottery center.

The art progressed to Germany where artists and artisans concentrated on the modeling of stoneware — from here came the invention of the salt glaze, which has proven to be very popular with modern day collectors.

Around 1650, Delft pottery became a thriving trade in the Netherlands, and much of the ware was exported. It was characterized by the use of a beautiful blue glaze decorating a white background. Later, Chinese and Japanese designs used green, red, and yellow, and finally black and rose were added.

In England, Staffordshire became the pottery center and from the eighteenth century produced novelties such as figurines and Toby jugs. Josiah Wedgwood made a wide variety of artistic, classic stoneware, and the technical processes practiced at his factory contributed greatly to the art.

Long before America was discovered, the Indians were making pottery of simple and original design. The Mound Builders of the Mississippi Basin show evidence of a high degree of culture. The Pueblo dwellers of the Southwest used the coil method, imitating in their pottery the appearance of their woven baskets. Later, their pottery became more graceful, in better proportion, and brightly decorated with color. The Mayan Indians were unaware of the potter's wheel, as were the other tribes, even though some of their altar stones were designed on a circular principle. Yet their pottery shows fine symmetry of form. Decorations were incised, stamped, or painted on with slip.

After the colonists settled in America, no later than 1650, several potteries in Virginia were turning out crude household wares. In South Carolina, in 1765, a superior clay was discovered and potted there, resulting in such a fine ware that Wedgwood considered it a threat. However, the pottery closed after operating only briefly and left no trace. Other potteries flourished for a short time in New York, Pennsylvania, Philadelphia, Massachusetts, and Connecticut. But since there was no popular market with the colonists who preferred the imported English wares, these also soon disappeared.

The first potteries of any permanence were situated in Ohio, where there was an abundance of the raw materials necessary to the making of pottery…dense clay beds and a plentiful supply of natural gas. Ohio had a growing transportation network that was steadily reaching further beyond its boundaries. Its population was growing, and from its heritage emerged native potters possessing the skill and know-how that resulted from long and diligent dedication to their craft.

In the late 1800s interest began to grow among the socially prominent young ladies in the delicate art of china painting. As interest continued, the art of ceramic decorating was no longer considered a mere pastime, but had developed into a fledgling art industry.

Scores of potteries sprang up in the immediate vicinity of Zanesville, Ohio, a small town situated on the Muskingum River…earning that place the title of "The Clay City." It was here, in 1891, that the pottery which holds our attention was founded: The Roseville Pottery Company.

The History of Roseville Pottery, From Beginning to End...

George F. Young, upon completion of his education in schools of his native county, entered into the field of education. Although he was held in high regard as a teacher, he left this profession after four years, moving to Zanesville in 1884, where he enrolled in a business college. Completing his course, he accepted the position of bookkeeper with the Singer Manufacturing Company and worked there for six years.

When the Roseville Pottery Company was incorporated on January 4, 1892, Young became general manager. Two years prior to this, the company had gone into stoneware, having purchased the abandoned facilities of the J. B. Owens Pottery of Roseville, Ohio, which had moved to Zanesville the previous year. With three coal-fired kilns they continued to produce the wares that had been made there by Owens — wares such as flowerpots, cuspidors, umbrella stands, and cooking utensils, none of which were marked.

Within a short time, Young had been promoted to secretary and, at the close of the first year, was made secretary and treasurer. Charles S. Allison was the first president of the company. J. F. Weaver was vice president, and Thomas Brown served in the capacity of treasurer before Young took the office. On the board of directors in addition to the officers were J. L. Pugh of Zanesville and J. N. Owens of Roseville. At the time of organization the capital stock of the company was $25,000.00. By 1905 the Muskingum County, Ohio, *Biography* states that the authorized capital had been increased to $300,000.00! It was under the continuing leadership and brilliant direction of Young that the

Roseville Pottery Company achieved its tremendous success, growing from this single plant employing 45 men in its infancy to a giant of commercial artware whose sales during World War II had reached a staggering $1,250,000.00. Young eventually became principal stockholder, and four generations of his family followed him in the management of the firm.

In 1898, their market growing and their facilities inadequate, the company expanded, purchasing the plant formerly owned by the Midland Pottery in Roseville; they thereby added three more kilns to the operation. In the same year the company moved their main office to Zanesville, Ohio. Although relocated, the company retained the use of the Roseville name. In Zanesville, they purchased the Clark Stoneware plant on Linden Avenue, formerly used by Peters and Reed. They enlarged and improved the facilities, erecting a three-story building of 50 x 156 feet and installed the latest machinery known to the trade. It was at this location two years later that the art pottery was produced.

In 1901 the company acquired the Muskingum Stoneware plant, formerly the Mosaic Tile Company, located at Muskingum Avenue and Harrison Streets in Zanesville. Here their German cookingware was made.

Roseville then controlled and operated four plants under the firm title, each with its own superintendent. They were equipped with a total of 30 periodic kilns and provided employment for more than 300 people.

Development of the Rozane Art Pottery
The vogue of ceramic decorating that had begun with

such enthusiasm in the latter 1800s had continued, and the interest it stirred was reason enough for several potteries to be established with the intent of capitalizing on the growing interest in art pottery. The Rookwood Pottery of Cincinnati, Ohio, founded in 1880, produced a line of art pottery on a dark blended background decorated with floral studies executed by hand under the glaze. The line was called Standard. The success of Rookwood attracted and prompted W. A. Long of Steubenville to enter the field with a similar line which he had developed after years of long and dedicated study. His line was called Lonhuda.

In 1893, after seeing the fine exhibits of art pottery on display at the World's Columbian Exposition, S. A. Weller — already a successful Zanesville potter of commercial wares — realized art pottery's potential market. In 1895 he negotiated with Long for the purchase of the Lonhuda Pottery and learned from him his methods of producing Lonhuda. Their association was brief and unpleasant; it was a disillusioned Long that took his methods and ideas with him to the J. B. Owens Pottery and there instructed artists and technicians in his procedure. Their art line was called Utopian and was, of course, a duplication of Lonhuda. Weller continued the production of Lonhuda, changing the name to Louwelsa and in a few years had become a wealthy man.

By 1900 Young felt that the Roseville Pottery Company was well enough equipped and staffed to contend with Weller for a share of the profits. He hired Ross Purdy to develop Roseville's first art line. His creation, a duplication of Lonhuda and Louwelsa, was called Rozane — a word coined from the firm's title and location. Rozane was a finely modeled line, ranging from shapes with full rounded bowls and long slender necks ending in deeply fluted rims to those of simplest classic proportions. Fine artists decorated the dark, blended backgrounds with nature studies, floral sprays, animals, and portraits of well-known personalities and American Indians. At the Historical Society in Columbus, Ohio, among the Roseville catalogs and records is a brochure of art studies which were available for reproduction on Rozane at the cost of less than 50¢ each. Some are easily recognized Rozane studies. While several smaller pieces might be finished in a day, larger pieces with more detailed painting could require several days. The first Rozane carried one of several marks, the most common being ROZANE or RPCo, both die impressed on the bottom of the piece. (See the chapter on trademarks for additional RPCo information.)

The smaller 5" to 6" Rozane Ware vases and bowls were offered for sale at prices from $5.00 to $12.00; the very large 24" to 30" floor vases sold from $50.00 to $90.00. For at least one sales promotion, the ware was presented as "Hollywood Ware" — the colored plate in the old catalogs that brought this to our attention bears the circular seal which has a narrow notched band around the circumference and the words Hollywood Ware in script within the circle.

Azurean was a line developed in 1902, similar to Weller's Blue Louwelsa. It was a blue and white underglaze decorated art ware on a blue blended background. Some pieces were marked with AZUREAN, die impressed, but most carry only the shape numbers and the letters RPCo.

In 1904 the Rozane Ware trademark was registered with the U. S. Patent Office. Patent #43,793 was issued to cover its use. The mark that was thereafter used to identify the Rozane art line was a circular ceramic wafer or seal with the words ROZANE WARE embossed over the outline of a long-stemmed rose.

Other Art Lines Added

While their commercial lines were probably their most profitable, the art lines drew attention to the pottery and gained for them prominence and prestige. In order to keep pace with his Zanesville competitors, Young had to respond to their new art lines with one from the Roseville pottery. As these new art lines were developed, the trade name Rozane became a generalized term used to indicate all art lines. In 1904 the original Rozane line was renamed Rozane Royal. In addition to the dark brown backgrounds, the Rozane Royal "lights," or pastel shades, were introduced. The same technique of underglaze slip painting was executed in soft gray, blue, green, ivory, and rose shades. The line was marked with the Rozane Ware ceramic seal with the particular line name, Royal, in block letters, enclosed in an attached arc below. Several other art lines bore this type of seal. (See chapter on trademarks.)

Capturing first prize at the St. Louis Expedition in 1904, Roseville's Rozane Mongol, a high gloss oxblood red line, gained recognition for the company and for its creator, John J. Herold. Herold, a native of Austria who was superintendent of the art department from 1900 to 1908, formulated the copper glaze after the fashion of the Chinese Sang de Boeuf, which was already considered a lost art at the time of the Chia Ching reign of the sixteenth century. Mongol shapes were typical of Chinese vase forms. Although it represented an important contribution to the field of art pottery, Mongol was not popular with the general public, and quite probably the company lost money on its production.

Occasionally a shape bearing the Rozane Mongol seal has been found in a blue or green high gloss glaze. In the picture section of this book you will see such a piece in a buff color. Roseville authorities term these colors trial glazes and point out that the artists and technicians were always encouraged to experiment. In the *Book of Pottery and Porcelain* (Warren Cox, Crown Publishers. Inc., 1970, Vol. 1, p. 556), we found a very interesting and enlightening theory discussed — one that may have been familiar to early Roseville artisans, perhaps to Herold himself. The text contains these words concerning the glazes and color of fine examples of K'ang Hsi Sang de Beoufs:

The inside of most specimens is finished with a buff crackled glaze…and in fact, specimens are found which are covered all over with this light glaze. Very often the red glaze slips down irregularly…leaving…buff areas…the red could only be brought out in the impurities existing in a muffle kiln.

He states that he could turn the reddest piece blue or green by refiring in a kiln that would drive off the impurities united with the copper.

In 1902 Weller introduced his Sicardo line — but not until 1905 was Roseville able to develop a similar line for the competitive market. John J. Herold is credited with the creation of Rozane Mara which was regarded as a successful imitation of the jealously guarded secret formula of Sicardo. Mara was a metallic luster line; shapes with simple embossed designs were decorated with iridescent shades of deep magenta to rose; those with a smooth surface were decorated with intricate patterns of the deep magenta interwoven with pearly gray or white tones. Mara was not in production nearly as long or in such large quantities as Sicardo, testimony to the difficulty involved in achieving satisfactory glazing, and most pieces found today are unmarked.

Roseville employed Gazo Fudji, a Japanese artist who had previously worked for Weller, to develop the Oriental art style of decoration that had continued to attract enthusiastic attention since being displayed in this country for the first time in 1876 at the Centennial Exposition in Philadelphia. The company's 1905 catalog shows the Rozane Woodland line, developed by Fudji. Woodland featured designs of naturalistic flowers and leaves, their outlines incised into the moist clay. Only the incised decorations were colored with a glossy enamel, the backgrounds left in the bisque state, and the inside glazed to hold water. On some pieces the bisque background was further decorated with stippling, done by hand with pins used to prick the soft clay. In the 1906 catalog, a type of similarly decorated ware was referred to as "Fujiyama" and was so marked with an underglaze stamp in black ink (see mark #8, page 21). According to Zanesville historian Norris Schneider, Fujiyama wares were decorated by Fudji himself. Today Fujiyama pieces are very scarce, but their unique designs and colors add credence to Gazo Fudji's decorating style.

Rozane Fudji was another line designed by Gazo Fudji. It first appeared in the company's 1905 catalog. It was similar to Woodland in that the colored designs decorated a bisque background which was usually a soft beige or a pale gray, shading to a more intense shade around the neck or at the base. Colored slip was painted on in unique, intricate patterns. Flowers were stylized, and solid lines arranged in Oriental forms were outlined with rows of dots. Beyond these were areas filled in with fields of wavy lines.

Even more limited in production, the Rozane Olympic line of 1905 was strikingly reminiscent of the ancient Greek red-figure wares. Scenes from Greek mythology were copied by means of a stencil; white figures outlined in black on a red background were accented by bands of the Greek key design. On some pieces, a caption descriptive of the scene was printed on the bottom in black ink along with the mark, ROZANE OLYMPIC POTTERY. Olympic and Mara are considered to be the rarest of the Roseville creations.

Rozane Egypto was an art line added in 1905. Christian Neilson, a native of Denmark and a graduate of the Royal Academy of Art at Copenhagen, was its creator. Egypto featured a matt glaze in old green and was modeled in low relief after examples of ancient Egyptian pottery. Today the suspended, two-tone glazes of Egypto, its predecessor Chloron, and its successor Matt Green rank highest among collectors who crave matt green glazes.

The pottery industry had always been plagued and production hampered by losses incurred in the firing process. Although usually discarded, the company attempted to market some of these pieces, claiming that the unexpected action of the fire had produced results of such a beautiful and artistic nature that the value of such a piece had actually increased. Each piece was inspected after firing and priced according to its individual merit.

New techniques were developed in the laboratories that represented considerable advancement in process and control. As a result, a new line, Rozane Crystalis, was developed. The crystalline glaze most often appears heavy and rough and rather sparsely studded with flat crystal flakes, although on some pieces, smooth surfaces are covered with beautiful frost-like crystals. The heavier, rough glaze seems to have been used on the Crystalis line shapes, shown in the 1906 catalog; the second type may have been applied to the standard Rozane shapes. Like Mongol, Rozane Crystalis met with only limited commercial success, although both represented valuable achievements to the art pottery industry. Crystalis is marked with the Rozane Ware seal or not at all.

Perhaps the most famous of the Roseville art lines was the Della Robbia line, introduced in 1905 by Frederick

found this enlightening notation: Broken means covered with breaks and vines. With this definition in mind, the line written in at the top of the sheet is more easily understood. Plate C is only one of many such pages that give formulas for some 222 different color effects; some are luster (unbroken) and some are marbleized (broken). The L. 5 finish, mentioned twice on the first page, was described as follows:

L. 5 Brown to Orange — not broken, 2 fires or more. Note below, L. 64 — same as L. 5, but lighter. L. 66 gives a formula for a dark blue and brown pebble finish. Another was for a pink on pink effect, with this notation penciled in… *"gives Carnelian glaze, undesirable."* Some "freaks" were noted, evidently a combination tried only once. On a page showing several vase shapes was yet another note: Vases and finishes sent to New York — Green, Blue, and Orange.

Plate B shows only one page of the sketches of Pauleo shapes. There were 18 shapes in all: one was a ginger jar; one large straight-edged vase was decorated (as were several others) with dragonflies — according to the notation below. Any art work was done overglaze on the luster cover, and the quality of the art work was not well developed.

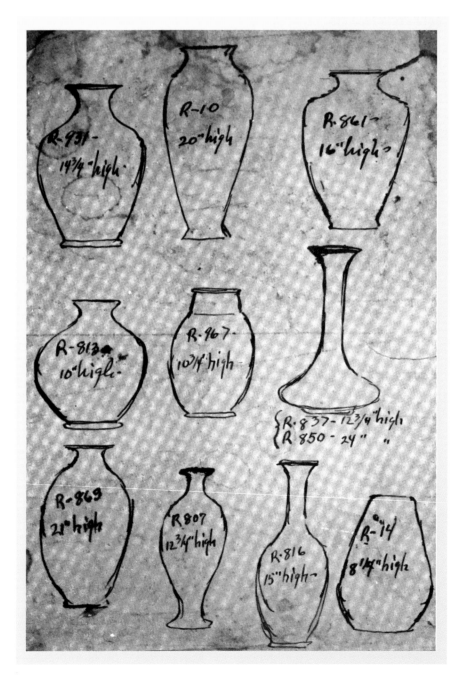

Plate B

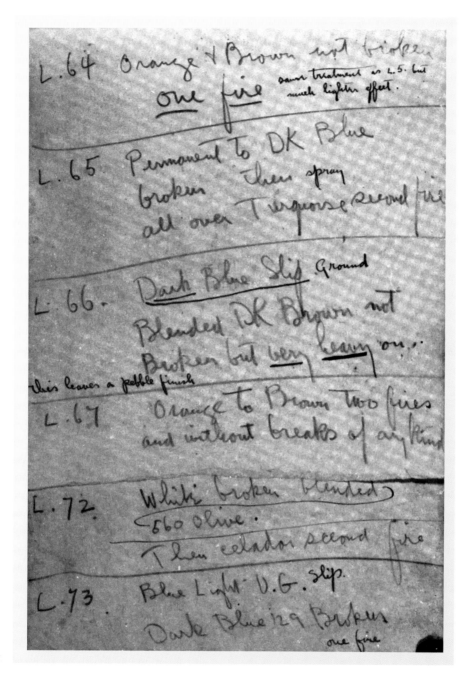

Plate C

Daily Reports of 1918 and 1919

The following paragraph and shaded text on pages 13 and 14 are taken from the Daily Reports of 1918 and 1919. Not every day's report is included, but the few shown here give insight to the operations at the pottery, and the problems that plagued them.

The average daily wage paid to the pottery employees in 1920 was around $3.50. The night watchmen earned $21.00 per week and worked 12 hours per shift. The night shift tunnel kiln man earned $24.00 for the same hours.

The following procedures were posted for the workers to observe at the end of the day shift:

> Girls: Quit working at 3:45, then clean up her place and retire to dressing room at 7 minutes until 4:00. Foremen will blow his whistle for retiring to dressing room.
>
> Men: Quit working at 4:30, then clean up his place and retire to top of steps at 20 minutes to 5:00. Foreman will blow his whistle for retiring to top of steps.

At a meeting of the department heads of the company, the following duties are ascribed to these individuals: Designers, Harry H. Rhead, designing and decorating, overseeing help, supervision of decorating rooms. Wade France, responsibility and shipment of orders, ordering of molds necessary, and making and settling of ware necessary to balance orders, hiring of men, and stock of packing room. W. C. Weaver, cooking ware, making finishes and quality of same, hiring of employees in said department. Harold Johns, charge of manufacturing department, responsible for hiring employees in the department. George Krause, glazing bodies and firing; and R. T. Young, all questions of wages, employment, and general supervision.

Jan. 15, 1918:

Trouble with cracking in the molds, baby plates are cracking in the bisque, teapot lids do not fit, new molds do not fit collars, blisters in the molds, lids for pots do not fit. Wade instructed to enforce rule, not enough care in preparing clay…too many lumps. Caused by hot air from exhaust fan.

Jan. 19, 1918:

Factory closed from war order until the 22nd. Wade…934 cracked baby plates, 960 good.

Jan. 21, 1918:

Cookware coming good, white bisque still cracking. George to change white body to avoid breakage in the kiln. (22nd entry shows less breakage after the change.)

Jan. 25, 1918:

Cookware too hard causing dark color. Shortage of teapots. Donatello bisque coming better. Teapots coming better. George complains of gas pressure, must have someone responsible all time. Rhead…blisters from top of kiln.

Jan. 20, 1918:

Streaky glazed cookware, caused by soft bisque.

Jan. 31, 1918:

Two more wheelmen needed. Ware coming without cracking, try to make ware lighter. Complaints of girls going from one department to another. Rule hereafter: no one to be employed who has worked in factory to be taken on until investigated by former foreman.

Feb. 1, 1918:

Baby plates bad, will try new style. Red pitchers crooked, claims due to handling green.

Feb. 4, 1918:

Will have 4 wheelmen in Tuesday. No one working today, Donatello 15 good and 16 bad, 3 cracked in bottom.

Feb. 6, 1918:

Started fire in tunnel kiln, no steam on the third floor. Weaver requires new wheel to make sixth wheelman.

Feb. 14, 1918:

Mostique still bad outside, George is trying new glaze. 573 jars handles blew off.

Feb. 15, 1918:

1,286 baby plates bad, 535, good.

Feb. 18, 1918:

Weaver in good shape, 5 wheelmen. Wade…cookware not hard enough, Johns needs new molds, George…new baby plate good.

Feb. 23, 1918:

New baby plate shape ready, Weaver short girls, too soft bisque. Johns 56 body not right.

May 23, 1918:

Rhead new baby plates fine, gloss very satisfactory. Weaver…6 wheels making 989 teapots daily. Clay is full of dirt. Wade…lids not fitting.

April 19, 1918:

Harold, ware coming good. Short one mold boy, sick. Will make 40% more nursery. Weaver short 4 boys, girls O. K. Unable to get men or boys. Wade…US 56 body bursting, Matt white blistering. Rhead can use man in nursery and white (ware). No. 1 Mug short. No record of bad man…all should be reported.

April 19, 1918:

Harold short 2 wheelmen and 5 girls. Wade…Donatello blistering and stain. Cause, not enough China clay in glaze. Weaver…2 men sick, girls O. K. Rhead, Gibbs still unable to work, trying to get another man.

May 8, 1918:

Weaver…One wheelman sick, short one mold carrier. Girls O. K. Ware fair. Harold, good shape. Wade…Donatello rough, everything else O. K. Redware coming slow.

June 10, 1918:

Harold…girls can decorate 36 8" Rozane (pattern) per day.

June 17, 1918:

Harold…2 wheelman off, mold boy drafted. Weaver short 4 more boys, clay foamy. Wade, short cookware and nursery.

June 18, 1918:

All in good shape, Harold…clay spongy. Offers to have change of clay of all kinds. Wade, bowls warped, 1 good out of 17 — Donatello — due to green sagers in the kiln.

June 20, 1918:

Rhead working one boy and girl under age, will abide by law and dismiss all under age.

July 5, 1918:

George changed glaze on Rozane. Harold…2 wheelmen off; one sick, one on vacation. Offinger…things looking much better, 3 girls short for week.

July 8, 1918:

Harold good shape, new Rozane better, bad bisque — set too green, try to avoid. Wade…cookware dirty, sager dirt and other things. Offinger…losing cookware in kiln. Not enough room to handle line and shop.

July 9, 1918:

Short girls for decorating Rozane. Short one wheelman.

July 29, 1918:

Rhead, kiln man not here, short several girls, bad ware caused by lack of supervisor. George thinks cookware not coming right. Unable to tell cause. Bad Rozane. Offinger getting along better. Still short. Wade…short nursery and cookware and Rozane. Short 5 girls.

George Young retired in 1918, turning the position of director over to his son, Russell T. Young. Frank Ferrell replaced Harry Rhead as art director that same year and continued in that capacity until 1954. The first of over 80 lines developed by Ferrell was Sylvan. As the name implies, the mood of Sylvan was characteristic of the deep woods; bisque backgrounds resembled tree bark while the enameled decorations were of leaves in a variety of species, owls, foxes, wild grapes, and many other variations. Dogwood, Ferrell's third line, was the first of the matte glazed Floral lines that were to become almost synonymous with the Roseville name.

During the years that Ferrell designed for Roseville new floral lines were added to production at the rate of at least two a year. Ferrella, introduced in 1930, was a classic line which carried Ferrell's name.

In 1932 Mrs. Anna Young, wife of George, became president of the Roseville Pottery Company, succeeding her son. The company incorporated and the firm name was changed to Roseville Pottery, Inc. The mark adopted for use during the early thirties was the name Roseville, in semi-script, cast indented into the ware. A number code added below the name indicated the shape number and the size to the nearest inch. Later, possibly as soon as 1937, the mark was changed from cast indented to cast raised, with the letters U. S. A. added.

The shaky economy of 1935 caused a drop in sales, and the Roseville company realized the need of a line they could sell in large volume. The Pine Cone samples that Ferrell had presented years before had been rejected. These discarded samples were again brought to the attention of the company and this time were accepted. Pine Cone eventually proved to be the most popular line ever produced at Roseville.

Following the death of Mrs. Young in 1937, her son-in-law, F. S. Clement, became president, a position he held until 1944. His successor was his son-in-law, Robert Windisch, who held that position until mid-year, 1953. For about seven months, Frederic J. Grant, former president of the Weller Company, took office temporarily and then was replaced by Windisch, who continued as president until the operation closed in 1954 (Donald E. Alexander, *Roseville Pottery for Collectors*).

From an all-time high of $1,250,000.00 in 1945, sales began a steady decline after WWII. There were many factors that contributed to this decline; the market was flooded with foreign imports produced and marketed at a fraction of the cost of domestic wares, and the sale of inexpensive plastic products flourished.

During the last years of production, the pottery introduced several lines with high gloss glazes attempting to revive public interest in their products. Several potteries in Ohio and West Virginia had successfully produced and marketed a type of high gloss ceramic kitchenware which proved to be very popular with the American housewives during the forties and into the fifties. Roseville introduced a line of this type called Mayfair. Although still retaining the artistic shapes and style for which they were famous, several pieces of the line — bowls, pitchers, teapots, etc. — were perhaps more utilitarian than in previous lines.

In 1948, following the suggestion of the president of the firm, Robert Windisch, a high gloss line called Wincraft revived shapes from some of the old successful lines. Pine Cone, Bushberry, Cremona, Primrose, and many other lines were represented. Vases with animal motifs were shown as were others with a contemporary flair. To the eyes of a buying public accustomed to the Roseville matte glaze, the Wincraft line with its high gloss seemed to be only a poor imitation; although many pieces were quite lovely and well suited to modern decor, it was never widely accepted.

In 1952, in a final attempt to re-establish a sound market, the company produced a line of oven-serve dinnerware in a modernistic design called Raymor. But the modern-day innovation of virtually indestructible melamine plastic dinnerware had attracted the attention of American housewives. Raymor met with no success and, as a result, all operations at the Roseville Pottery were discontinued. In November 1954, the plant was sold to the Mosaic Tile Company.

The giant pottery that grew and flourished for 64 years has long since disappeared into the haze of the past, trampled by the march of progress...but to those who enjoy the beauty they created, the Roseville Pottery will be forever remembered.

A Visit to Some Zanesville Potteries

We went first to the Roseville potteries, which occupy a large group of buildings, wherein is manufactured a great variety of wares, including washstand sets, jardinieres, and art ware. Over three hundred persons are employed at this plant, and about five thousand pieces of finished ware are turned out every day.

As our time was limited, and we were both very fond of art pottery, my friend and I visited only the rooms in which the art ware is manufactured.

Our guide led us from room to room, showing and explaining to us the various processes through which the clay passes.

We learned that the Ohio clays naturally run to golden browns and yellows that can be preserved unaltered through the intense heat of the firing to which the ware is subjected. Most of the potteries use clay from the neighboring hills, but to produce certain kinds of ware and certain color effects, other ingredients are added; sometimes clays from other sources are used entirely or mixed with the native clays.

The abundant supply of natural gas at Zanesville is a potent factor in the manufacturing of all kinds of pottery. By its use, degrees of heat are attained that would be impossible by other methods of firing, and the buildings are kept clean and free from dust.

Led by our guide, we viewed with interest the processes through which the clay is taken, from the time it reaches the factory, fresh from the neighboring hills, until it is transformed into a thing of beauty, fit to grace an artistic home.

The clay is pulverized and thoroughly washed, filtered, and mixed with water, to a certain consistency. It is then either by hand or machine pressed into a mold made of plaster of Paris. This mold absorbs the water, making a body of clay next to the mold. After three or four minutes, the liquid that remains is poured out. The shell thus left is the future vase. It goes to the finisher who sponges and smooths off all defects.

The underglaze art ware is sprayed with a clay liquid in mineral colors, and the blending is done by the young girls in charge of this branch of the work. We were allowed to stand and watch the decorators at work, painting from nature or copy in mineral colors, giving to each article with skillful fingers its own individual crown of beauty.

After being decorated, the piece is taken to the dry room, where it stays until the water has all evaporated, and then is placed in the kiln.

We were surprised to find how large the kilns are, some of them being twenty feet high inside. The men have to climb on ladders to reach the top of the tall columns of saggers, or boxes of clay which contain the the precious ware. At the right time, after the ordeal by fire, each article is dipped in a liquid glass solution called glaze, and after this, fired for the second time and is then a finished product.

We were told that we had seen the usual process of manufacturing art ware, but variations of this and different processes are used, to produce other effects, and that the artist chemists are allowed to experiment, and often achieve wonderful results.

The greatest care in every detail must be exercised in order to secure perfection.

Most of the decorators were women, and I observed women and girls at work in many other rooms. Such employment must be very pleasant, congenial, and suitable, bringing them into constant contact with beauty, in form and color, and it demands the care, patience, and attention to detail which women are fitted by nature to give to their work.

The art ware that is made at Roseville is known by the general name of Rozane Ware. In the large sales rooms we saw the different kinds, each having its own peculiar charm.

The first style was developed in the natural golden browns and yellows of the native clays, and is called Rozane Royal.

Our attention was attracted to a collection of vases, varying in shape, in a solid color, a deep rich, beautiful red without decorations, and we found we were viewing a unique and new variety, the Rozane Mongol, resembling the far-named Doulton ware of England.

Near this stood a group of articles in soft shades of old green, reproductions in shape and decoration of antiques of Egyptian art. The attractive and restful color and the graceful modeling of decoration were harmonious and pleasing. My friend considered this ware ideal for holding flowers and said she could imagine how beautiful nasturtiums or carnations would look in Rozane Egypto vases.

More ornamental and striking is the Rozane Mara, whose iridescent surface seems to hold a stray rainbow imprisoned in its shining depths. The shifting opal tints, varying in tone, flushing to deepest rose, produce a beautiful play of color.

We were highly pleased with Rozane Woodland, whose exceptional beauty elicits instant praise. Gray, yellow, or brown shaded backgrounds are decorated with enameled or modeled designs, usually in foliage in brown or russet autumnal hues. A Japanese artist, Gazo Foudji, formerly of Paris, does the original and exquisite work in his private studio at Roseville.

Having spent all the time at our disposal, viewing the art ware, we were obliged to hasten away from the Roseville potteries, without devoting any attention whatever to the other lines of ware manufactured there.

Lura Milburn Cobb
The Southwesterner's Book, Dec. 1905

Several of these artists' initials correspond with some of those from Owens, and it seems likely that they would have migrated to Roseville when art pottery production was discontinued at Owens in 1906. Many well-known Roseville artists did in fact once work at Owens: Virginia Adams, A.F. Best, John Butterworth, Charles Chilcote, Frank Ferrell, John Herold, Mae Timberlake, and no doubt others. It is doubtful that artists such as Fannie Bell, Edith Bell, or Cecelia Bloomer (all known to have been at Owens) would not have continued to pursue their careers elsewhere during a time when the production of art pottery was at its peak. Some of our "unknown" artists' cyphers could very well be theirs.

Elizabeth Ayers

Jenny Burgoon

Virginia Adams (or full last name)

E. C. (unknown) Della Robbia

C. B. (unknown) Crocus

Charles Chilcote

E. B., E. R. B. (unknown) Della Robbia

Dibowski – no signature available

F. B., F. A. B. (unknown) Della Robbia

Anthony Dunlavy

G. B. (unknown) Della Robbia

Charles Duvall – no signature available

M. B.

Katy Duvall Della Robbia

A.F. Best

M. F.

Gazo Fudji — *Fujiyama*

Gussie Gerwick — *G ; G Gerwick*

Golde Della Robbia — *-G- -Golde-*

Madge Hurst — *MH.*

William Hall Rozane — *W.H.*

John Herold — *J. H.*

Josephine Imlay — *J.I. ; J Imlay*

Harry Larzelere — *HL*

Claude Leffler Azurean, Rozane — *CLL £ Leffler*

F. M. — *F. M.*

L. McGrath – no signature available

Mignon Martineau — *M*

C. Mitchell Rozane — *C Mitchell*

Lily Mitchell — *LM ; Mitchell*

B. Myers — *B. MYERS*

Walter Myers — *W. MYERS*

M. N. (unknown)
Rozane

MN

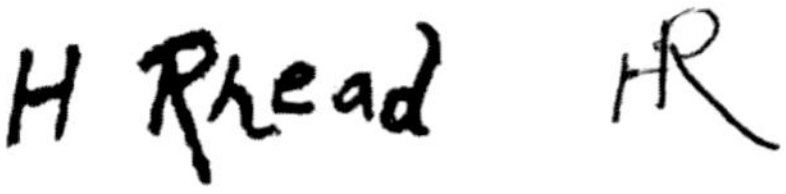

Lois Rhead – no signature available

C. Neff
Rozane
(several Neff signatures
began with the letter C)

C NEFF

Helen Smith

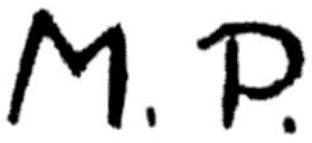

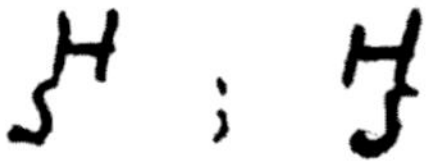

ʃH ; ʧ

Grace Neff

G. NEFF

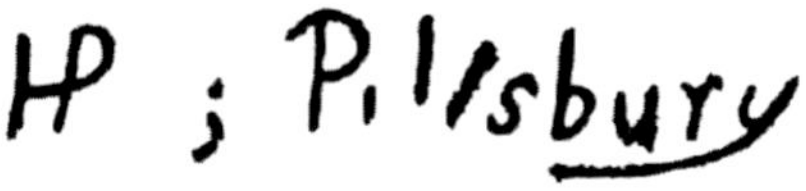

Fred Steel

F steele

Mary Pierce

M. P.

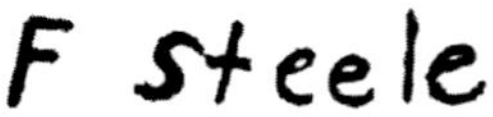

C.S. (unknown)
Decorated Matt

ʃ

Hester Pillsbury

HP ; Pillsbury

E. T. (unknown)
Woodland

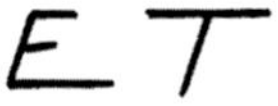

E T

Frederick H. Rhead

F Rhead ; F. R.
F HR

Mae Timberlake

M. T.

Harry Rhead

H Rhead   HR

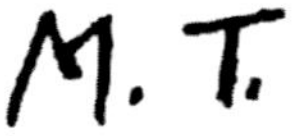

Arthur Williams

AW

After 1900, when the Rozane art line was added to the commercial wares already in production, the company established a system of identification using a number code. Each series of numbers indicated the particular type of ware being produced, and each number in sequence within the series represented a shape. The numbering system was discontinued after about 1910, and not until the cast indented (impressed) mark of the early thirties was it resumed. Incorporated in the case-indented mark and the cast-raised (embossed) mark that followed around 1937 were the shape number and the size to the nearest inch.

Other letters and numbers found in ink or pencil on the bottom of many pieces of the commercial art lines were used to identify specific workers doing a specialized job, such as molding, cleaning, decorating, or inspection. These were simply an aid to quality control.

A wide variety of marks were used during the years of production at the Roseville Pottery. Although some lines were marked in more than one manner, often the mark can be an important factor to consider where proper identification of a line is in question…i.e., a novice could distinguish Florane (RV mark) from the 1940s Rozane (marked Roseville, U. S. A. in

relief) simply by observing the mark. As he becomes more familiar with the pottery, he would of course recognize either line simply by shape or by the slight variation in the colors. Similarly, Panel is obviously marked RV, and Silhouette, Roseville U. S. A. in relief.

The dates given for the marks below indicate the period of greatest use; however it is generally felt that the use of some marks extended beyond the time that a new one was developed.

Of the many unmarked pieces found today, some were never marked in any way; others originally bore a paper label. If there is evidence of an applied ceramic seal having been removed or mutilated, be advised that the piece in question was a second, sold only through Roseville's outlet, not through the retail market.

Items marked RRPCO, Roseville, Ohio, were made by the Robinson-Ransbottom Pottery Company of Roseville, Ohio. RRPCO is not a Roseville Pottery mark. During the 1970s, Robinson-Ransbottom made a line of jardinieres and pedestals, flowerpots, and vases in a green/brown running glaze reminiscent of items made in the early 1900s. Some were embossed with flowers, others with geometric panels.

MARK 1

ROZANE RPCo   RPCo

Die impressed mark used from 1900 – 1904 – (?)

MARK 2

Paper sticker, 1900 (?), very rare.

MARK 3

AZUREAN   AZUREAN RPCo

Die impressed, 1902 – (?)

MARK 4

Paper label used on assortment of Rozane shapes with floral and fruit studies that differed slightly from the norm. Hollywood Ware, ca. 1905.

MARK 5

Paper sticker, printed in red ink; applied at the pottery; indicated stock number and retail price.

MARK 6

Applied ceramic seal, late 1904 – late 1906.

MARK 7

Applied ceramic seal with line name in chevron, late 1904 – early 1906.

MARK 8

Black ink stamp, 1906

MARK 9

ROZANE
"OLYMPIC"
POTTERY

Black ink stamp or printed, often includes description
of mythological scene, 1905.

MARK 10

Impressed or ink stamp, late 1904.

MARK 11

R or R

Usually ink stamped, 1910 – 28; re-introduced
in 1930s for utility ware and Juvenile.

MARK 12

ROSEVILLE
POTTERY CO.
ZANESVILLE, O.

Red ink stamp, ca. 1900 – (?)

MARK 13

Applied ceramic seal, 1914 – (?)

MARK 14

Impressed, 1915

MARK 15	MARK 16
ROSEVILLE ROZANE WARE POTTERY	
Ink stamp, 1917	Black paper sticker, 1914 – 33.

MARK 17	MARK 18
	Roseville 915-5" Roseville U.S.A.
Silver or gold foil sticker, 1930 – 37	Impressed, 1932 – 37

MARK 19

Be aware that there are many copies of Roseville coming in from China with the Roseville name as shown on the left without the U.S.A. To be authentic, this mark must contain the letters U.S.A.

Roseville U.S.A.   R U.S.A.   R U.S.A.

In relief, 1937 – 53

MARK 20	MARK 21	MARK 22
	ROSEVILLE L-23 PASADENA PLANTER U.S.A.	152L Raymor by Roseville U.S.A. OVEN PROOF PAT. PEND.
In relief, 1951	In relief, 1952	In relief, 1952

Note: All dates are approximate.
* indicates catalog reprints

Antique Matt Green, before 1916. Simple shades in matte green glaze with areas that have a burnished or rusty appearance.

Apple Blossom, 1948. Spray of white blossoms on backgrounds of pink, blue, green, brown tree branches form graceful handles.

Artcraft, 1930s. Art Deco, simple and elegant shapes; warm mottled tan or blue-green similar to Earlam glaze, rarely also found in red. Vertically layered buttresses atop shoulder at mid-point of body.

Artwood, early 1950s. A high-gloss line in mottled colors of yellow shading to brown, green to brown, and gray to wine. The focus of the design featured shaped openings containing an element from nature, most often a tree or a branch.

Autumn, before 1916. Creamware decorated by means of pouncing. Shades of cream to yellow depicting trees and countryside.*

Aztec, 1905. Simple decorations formed with thin threads of clay using a squeeze-bag technique.

Azurean, 1902. Blue and white underglaze art ware on a blue blended background.

Azurine, Orchid, and Turquoise, 1920. Simple shapes, very similar to Lustre line, high gloss, lustrous glaze.

Baneda, 1933. Decorative band of leaves, pods, and blossoms on backgrounds of red, green, and more rarely, blue.

Banks, turn of the century. Novelties and banks in the forms of a cat, Uncle Sam, pigs, dog, buffalo, and eagle; poorly hand decorated under glaze.*

Bittersweet, late 1940s. Orange pods and green with twig handles on backgrounds of mint green, gray, or yellow.

Blackberry, 1933. Band of berries, vines, and leaves in natural color, on green rough-textured background.

Bleeding Heart, 1940. Pink blossoms and green foliage on backgrounds of shaded pink or blue.

Blue Ware, 1920s. Teapots, tall pots, and mugs in cobalt blue decorated primarily in stark white slipwork.

Burmese, early 1950s. Oriental faces decorate such items as wall plaques, book-ends, candle holders, center bowls, etc. Other items are simple with no decoration. Colors are green, black, and white.

Bushberry, 1948. Leaves and berries on bark-like backgrounds of green, blue, or russet.

Cameo, 1920. Antique ivory bands with embossed figures and trees, or vertical panel with peacock, on dark green or ivory backgrounds.*

Cameo II, ca. 1916 – 1918 (Unofficial name). Previously unidentified line of color-tinted creamware decorated with scrollwork and deeply fluted columns centered with cameos of cherub heads. Shapes include a double-bud vase "gate," flowerpot/saucer, hanging basket, wall pocket, basket, window box, ashtray, assortment of vases and bowls, and a jardiniere and pedestal set. Limited production; a forerunner to Donatello. See Book II for more information and photos.

Capri, early 1950s. Modern shapes; moderately priced line geared toward lower-end market. Vases, baskets, ashtrays and planters in a variety of glaze colors and effects.

Carnelian I, 1910 – 15. Its ornate handles are characteristic of the line. The glaze is a smooth matte with a drip glaze in a darker shade: light with medium blue, aqua blue with turquoise, pink with green, and green with antique gold.

Pine Cone floor vase, Roseville #913-18 impressed.
Blue, $4,000.00 – 4,500.00. Brown, $2,500.00 – 3,000.00.
Green, $2,000.00 – 2,500.00.

Carnelian II, 1920s. Shapes are very simple, the glaze is heavy and textured; turquoise, rose, black, purple and yellow glazes are intermingled and show some dripping.

Ceramic Design, before 1916. Creamware, usually embossed designs in colors of yellow, green, and black. However, catalogs show a repetitive border-type pattern, applied by the pouncing technique in bright colors, which is referred to as Persian-type ceramic design.

Cherry Blossom, 1933. Blue with pink lattice, yellow with brown lattice, sprigs of cherry blossoms and twigs.

Chloron, 1904. Solid matte green glaze, sometimes with sections in ivory, modeled in high relief after early Roman and Greek pottery artifacts.* Bottoms are buff colored; they may be matt or glossy.

Clemana, 1936. Basketweave backgrounds of green, blue, or tan, with stylized blossoms and leaves.

Clematis, 1944. Clematis blooms on backgrounds of autumn brown, ciel blue, or forest green.

Colonial, 1900s. Glossy spongeware in shades of blue, with gold highlights on embossed detail at base of handles.*

Columbine, 1941. Floral and leaf arrangement on shaded backgrounds of tan, blue, or pink.

Corinthian, 1923. Deep vertical ivory fluting with green in recessed areas; green band decorated with twisted grapevines, leaves and fruit in natural colors; further embellished by a finely modeled narrow band in ivory and green.

Cornelian, pre-1900s. Glossy spongeware in shades of yellow and brown, accented with random areas of gold spray.*

Cosmos, 1939. Delicate flowers and greenery on suggestion of a band, textured background colors are blue, green, or tan.

Creamware, before 1916. A type of highly refined earthenware body, very light in color; the basis for many decal-decorated lines, steins, smoker's sets, etc.

Cremo, 1916. Shades from rose at the top, through yellow to dark green at the bottom. Characterized by vertical, evenly spaced, swirling stems with single blossom in blue.*

Cremona, 1927. Floral motif varies; some pieces have single tall stem with small blossoms and several arrowhead leaves; others are wreathed with leaves similar to Velmoss; a third variety is a web of delicate vines; characteristic glaze has a buttermilk, or curdled effect; backgrounds are light green mottled with pale blue, or pink with creamy ivory. There is also a medium green, with less texture than the other colors, and you may find still other shades.

Crocus, ca. 1905 – 10. Very similar to Aztec, but with slipwork rather than squeeze-bag decoration; glazes are shiny.

Crystal Green, 1930s. Modeled with a floral sprig similar to Velmoss II but differing in that the sprig extends upward from the base. Handles are ornate, done in Ferrell's typical style. If marked, Velmoss II carries the foil sticker, while the mark for Crystal Green is Roseville impressed and a shape number.

Crystalis, Rozane, 1906. Unique shapes, some with extreme handles; many are three-footed; textured glaze with scattered crystal flakes, or standard Rozane shapes with smooth surface and grown crystals, rare. Also see text.*

Dahlrose, 1928. Mottled tan background with band formed by ivory flowers and green leaves.

Dawn, 1937. Simple incised floral decoration; long slender petals, no leaves; backgrounds are pink, yellow, or green.

Decorated and Gold Traced, before 1916. Same as Gold Traced, but with added floral motif, similar to Persian. Listed in this manner in old price list.*

Decorated Art, 1900. Art Nouveau style jardinieres and pedestals, etc., featuring flowers, scrollwork, and elaborate modeling, sometimes incorporating lions' heads.

Decorated Landscape, early line. Large jardinieres and pedestals with brown backgrounds in high gloss, decorated with trees in the style of Frederick Rhead.

Decorated Matt, ca. 1910. Large jardinieres, umbrella stands, possibly other items decorated in soft pastel slipwork on pastel backgrounds.

Decorated Utility Ware, 1929. Creamware with high gloss, some decorated with wide bands of green or orange, narrowly piped in black; another type is decorated with slender blue leaves and orange berries.

Della Robbia, Rozane, 1905 – 06. Naturalistic or stylized designs executed by hand using the sgraffito method. Also see text.*

Dogwood I, 1919 – 20. Smooth green background with white dogwood blossoms on black branches.

Dogwood II, 1926. Textured green background with white dogwood blossoms on brown branches.

Donatello, 1915. Deep vertical fluting in ivory and green, on either side of a brown band with embossed ivory cherubs and trees. Catalog also shows gray and ivory combination. Also see text.

30½", Dahlrose jardiniere and pedestal,
unmarked, $1,800.00 – 2,250.00.

Donatella Tea Sets, before 1916. This term referred to tea sets, consisting of teapot, sugar, and creamer, in a variety of patterns, such as Landscape, Ceramic, Forget-Me-Not, Medallion, and others.*

Dutch, before 1916. Creamware with decals of varied scenes with Dutch children; trimmed with narrow blue piping at the rim.

Earlam, 1930. Very simple shapes glazed in mottled turquoise or tan with subtle contrasting shadings. Turquoise pieces lined in tan. Included in this line were many crocus pots.

Early Pitchers, before 1916. High gloss, utility line of pitchers with various embossed scenes. Shown are The Bridge, The Cow, The Boy, The Golden Rod, The Wild Rose, The Mill, The Grape, No. I Holland, No. II Holland, Teddy Bear, Iris, Tulip, Landscape, and Owl.*

Egypto, Rozane, 1905. Matte glaze green, modeled from examples of ancient Egyptian pottery. All Egypto must have the ceramic Rozane seal.

Elsie, the Cow, 1950s. Advertising line made for Borden's; consists of mug, cereal bowl, and plate with embossed decorations of Elsie the Cow; in high gloss rust glaze.

Falline, 1933. Blended and shaded backgrounds of primarily blue or tan; evenly curving panels are separated by vertical "pea-pod" decorations.

Ferella, 1930. Tan or rose-red curdled glaze effect; decorated with bands of stylized shells and cut-outs around the rim and base.

Florane, 1920s. Shaded matte glaze of caramel tan to very dark brown on simple shapes, often from the Rosecraft line.

Florane II, early 1950s. Free-forms and simple shapes with a contemporary flair; blue, lime green, and tan exteriors lined with tan.

Florentine, 1924 – 28. Brown bark textured panels alternating with vertical stripes embossed with cascades of leaves and berries, also brown. Found occasionally in ivory with green cascades and brown textured panels.

Florentine II, ca. 1950s. Similar to the ivory Florentine, but without cascades on the dividing panels, marked Roseville, U. S. A. in relief.

Forget-Me-Not, before 1916. Creamware decorated with decal of small blue or lavender flowers, with gold piping.

Foxglove, 1942. Tall spires of flowers in delicate colors, on backgrounds of shaded pink, blue, and green.

Freesia, 1945. Floral clusters, blade-like leaves on shaded backgrounds of tropical green, Delft blue, and tangerine.

Fudji, Rozane, 1905. Bisque backgrounds in tones of gray or beige, decorated with colored slip in unique, intricate patterns. Also see text.

Fudjiyama, 1906. Similar to Woodland but done by the designer of the line, Gazo Fudji, himself.

Fuchsia, 1938. Vine with serrated leaves and delicate blooms on highlighted backgrounds of blue, tan, or forest green.

Futura, 1924. Very diversified line; some forms are angular, suggesting a geometric or Art Deco feeling; some suggest lines of the future, Pine Cone, Teasel, and others; some are decorated with leaves in various colors. Typical glaze is matte, although an occasional piece may be high-gloss.*

Garden Pottery, 1931. Stoneware, pots, jardiniere, and birdbaths with a variety of embossed decorations.*

Gardenia, 1940s. White gardenia, green leaves, on slightly textured, shaded backgrounds of seafoam, golden tan, and silver haze gray.

German Cooking Ware, 1912. Utilitarian line; brown lined in white, decorated with a border of scallops at the top. This line contained such items as coffeepots, teapots, pitchers, custard or bean pots, casseroles, shirred egg cups, pudding dishes, mixing bowls, etc.

Gold Traced, before 1916. Candle holders, candelabra, etc., in white with delicate gold patterns.*

Holland, before 1916. Dutch figures are embossed on an ivory background shaded green around the rim and base.*

Holly, before 1916. Creamware with decal of holly leaves and red berries with narrow piping at the rim.

Home Art, early 1900s. Simple shapes — jardinieres, pedestals, umbrella stands, etc. — in both dark and light Rozane glazes decorated with decals either by the hobbyist or on special order by the company.

Imperial I, 1916. Pretzel-twisted vine and stylized grape leaves decorate rough textured background in green and brown. Style of modeling is rather crude.

Imperial II, 1924. Much variation within the line. There is no common characteristic, although many pieces are heavily glazed, and colors tend to run and blend.*

Individual tea sets, before 1916. Decorated creamware in such various patterns as Ceramic Design, Medallion, Dutch, Forget-Me-Not, Landscape, in sets containing the teapots, sugar, and creamer.

Iris, 1939. White iris, green blades on blended backgrounds of blue, pink, or caramel tan.

Ivory II, 1937. White matte glaze shapes from earlier lines such as Orian, Velmoss, Russco, Donatello, Tourmaline, and others. Also included in the line is a figurine of a nude with flowing drapery, and another of a sleeping dog, also in white.*

Ixia, 1930s. Delicate floral cluster on stem; shaded background colors are yellow, pink, and green. Closed, pointed handles are characteristic.

Jeanette, before 1916. Creamware decorated with decal of standing girl in period costume.

Jonquil, 1931. White jonquil clusters and green leaves on textured brown background, lined in green.

Juvenile, 1916 – 35. Creamware, decorated by means of pouncing (perforated waxed pattern) in various motifs — chicks, bunnies, on matte glaze; duck with hat, sunbonnet girl, rabbit with jacket, pig with hat, dancing cat with parasol, etc., on high gloss.*

Landscape, 1910. Creamware decorated with decals of windmills and sailing boats, in blue and brown.

La Rose, 1924. Ivory background wreathed with swags of green vines caught up with small red roses. Beaded border at rim.

Laurel, 1934. Background colors are russet or old gold, both accented with black; or in shades of green. Wide panels symmetrically divided by three impressed vertical ribs are wreathed with laurel branches.

Lombardy, 1924. Solid colors of green or blue are characterized by narrow, perpendicular panels tapering to a common point at center bottom.*

Lotus, 1952. Pointed spires of stylized leaves surround each piece. High gloss glaze in combinations of maroon with beige; brown with beige; and blue with beige.

Luffa, 1934. Backgrounds are green or brown, with horizontal wavy lines, decorated by a border of several small flowers and two large leaves with long points extending downward.

Lustre, 1921. Simple shapes with lustrous glaze in pink, orange, blue, etc.*

Magnolia, 1943. Magnolia blossoms on black stem, textured backgrounds are green, blue, and tan.

Mara, Rozane, 1905. Metallic lustre line, similar to Sicardo. Intricate patterns on smooth surface in magenta and silver gray; simple embossed designs in iridescent shades of rose to magenta. Also see text.

Matt Color, 1920s. Simple paneled designs of various types, in colors of light blue, turquoise, yellow, and pink. Later issued in high gloss in a variety of colors.*

Matt Green, before 1916. Matte green glaze on smoking set, jardinieres, fern dishes, hanging baskets, planters; some smooth with no pattern; some embossed with leaves, children's faces, spaced evenly around the top. Entire piece is glazed; green continues down outside and wraps around base to cover entire vase.

Mayfair, early 1950s. High gloss glaze, utilitarian line, in beige, brown with tan, dark green with tan, and lime.

Medallion, before 1916. Creamware decorated with delicate gold decals around rims, and evenly spaced rose or green mercury head medallions.

Ming Tree, 1949. High gloss glaze in mint green,

turquoise, or white is decorated with ming branch; handles are formed from gnarled branches.

Mock Orange, 1950. Small cluster of white blossoms and green leaves on backgrounds of pink, yellow, or mint green.

Moderne, 1930s. Art Deco modeling, simple decorations, in tan, green, and blue.*

Mongol, Rozane, 1904. High gloss blood-red line on typical Chinese vase forms. Also see text.

Montacello, 1931. Black and white stylized trumpet flower evenly spaced, extending from brown ribbon-like band, turquoise background with tan blush, brown with tan.

Morning Glory, 1935. Delicately colored blossoms and twining vines in white or green with blue.

Moss, 1936. Green moss hanging over brown branch with green leaves, backgrounds are pink to green, orange to green, or blue.

Mostique, 1915. Indian designs of stylized flowers and arrowhead leaves, slip decorated on bisque, glazed interiors. Occasional bowl glazed on outside as well.

Normandy, 1924. Green and white vertical fluting over bottom portion, wide brown band, decorated with ivory looped vines, pink grapes, and green leaves around rim.

Novelty Steins, before 1916. Line of creamware mugs,

Della Robbia teapot, Morning (rooster on reverse) and Night (owl), 6½", $2,500.00 – 3,500.00.

decorated with decals with whimsical scenes and messages.*

Old Ivory, before 1916. (Also called Ivory Frieze.) Intricate patterns in high relief of stylized grapevines or flowers; also was made in delicate colors of pink, blue, and green. When these tints were used, the color was wiped from the areas in highest relief and was usually referred to as green tint, blue tint, etc.

Olympic, Rozane, 1905. White figures outlined in black on a red background accented by bands of the Greek key design, depicting scenes from Greek mythology. Also see text.

Opac Enamels, 1900. Simple jardiniere in plain colors of yellow, rose, and green.

Orian, 1935. Characterized by handles formed of blade-like leaves with suggestion of berries at base of handle…high gloss glaze; turquoise or tan with darker drip glaze forming delicate band around rim, or in plain yellow with no overdrip, also some red.

Pasadena Planter, 1952. High gloss pink or black, with border at rim formed by white drip glaze; line consists of a variety of shapes of flower containers or planters in modern shapes.

Pauleo, 1914. Prestige line of 222 color combinations and two glaze types, lustre or marbleized. See text.

Peony, 1942. Floral arrangement with green leaves on textured, shaded backgrounds in yellow with brown; pink with blue; and green.

Persian, 1916. Creamware decorated by means of pouncing technique, in bright colors, water lily and pad most common motif, although a variety of others were also used.

Pine Cone, 1935. Graceful needles and pine cones decorate backgrounds of brown, green, or blue. Handles are formed from branches. Pink background extremely rare.

Poppy, 1930s. Shaded backgrounds of blue, gray, green, or pink with decoration of poppy flower and green leaves. Rarely found in tan as well.

Primrose, 1932. Cluster of single blossoms on tall stems, low pad-like leaves, backgrounds are blue, tan, or pink.

Raymor, 1952. Modernistic design, oven-serve dinnerware made in colors of tan, ivory, gray, dark green, black, and medium green.

Raymor Modern Artware, 1950s. Mid-century high style vases and bowls in semi-matte colors of black and tan. Each piece is marked with the line designation.

Rosecraft, 1920s. Simple shapes in glossy glazes, colors are yellow, dark blue, light blue, and rose.*

Rosecraft Black, 1916. Simple shapes, high gloss black glaze.*

Rosecraft Blended, 1920s. Simple Rosecraft shapes glazed in soft pastel mottled glazes.

Rosecraft Hexagon, 1924. Shapes are six-sided, simple medallion design with long slender stylized leaf extending downward. Colors are dark green; brown with orange; catalog also shows blue.

Rosecraft Panel, 1920. Background colors are dark green or dark brown, decoration embossed within the recessed panels are of natural or stylized floral arrangements or female nudes.

Rosecraft Vintage, 1924. Dark brown backgrounds with band at shoulder formed by repetitive arrangement of leaves, vines, and berries, in colors of beige to orange.

Royal Capri, early 1950s. Occasional pieces with modern forms, having a textured gold surface.

Rozane, 1900 – 05. Dark blended backgrounds; slip decorated underglaze art ware. Also see text.

Rozane, 1917. Honeycomb backgrounds in ivory, light green, pink, yellow, blue; decorated with green leaves and clusters of roses in delicate tints.

Rozane Pattern, 1940s. Solid or blended matte glazes on simple shapes. Shaded browns, greens, or blues.

Rozane Royal, Royal Lights, 1900 – 05. With the addition of the new art lines, in 1904, the name Rozane was changed to Rozane Royal, to distinguish the underglaze artist decorated line from the other lines. Also at this time, the Royal Lights were added; slip decorated underglaze in lighter shades of gray, blue, pink, etc. See text.

Russco, 1930s. Octagonal rim openings, stacked handles, narrow perpendicular panel front and back. One type glaze is solid matte color; another is matte color with lustrous crystalline over glaze, some of which show actual grown crystals.

Savona, 1924 – 28. High gloss glaze of salmon pink, light blue, or lime green on finely modeled classic shapes, some with deeply fluted areas around the base or near the top, with the remaining smooth areas decorated with cascading grapevines in high relief.*

Silhouette, 1952. Recessed area silhouettes nature study or female nudes. Colors are rose, turquoise, rust, and white.

Smoker sets, before 1916. Tobacco jars, ashtrays, etc., on a tray in a variety of patterns, such as Dutch, Holland, Matte Green, Ivory Frieze, and Indian, and the tint colors.

Snowberry, 1946. Brown branch with small white berries and green leaves embossed over spider web design in various background colors, blue, green, and rose.

Special, early 1900s. Art Nouveau jardinieres, pedestals, vases, tankards, and mugs, often featuring stenciled grapes on light shaded backgrounds; Rozane shapes.

Stein sets, before 1916. Creamware tankards and steins decorated with various decals of Dutch, Eagle, Elk, Moose, Indian, Monk, and K of P. Also included were Holland, Ivory Frieze, and the tint colors of green, pink, yellow, and blue. Others were hand painted.

Sunflower, 1930. Tall stems support yellow sunflowers whose blooms form a repetitive band. Textured background shades from tan to dark green at base.

29", Jonquil jardiniere and pedestal,
unmarked, rare. $2,500.00 – 3,000.00.

Sylvan, 1918. Tree bark textured background, incised with decorations of maple leaves, dogs, chickens, foxes, owls, ivy, and acorns. Interiors are glazed.*

Teasel, 1936. Embossed decorations of long stems, gracefully curving, with delicate spider-like pods. Colors and glaze treatments vary from monochrome matte to crystalline. Colors are beige to tan; medium blue, highlighted with gold; pale blue; and russet.

Thorn Apple, 1930. White trumpet flower with leaves reverses to thorny pod with leaves. Colors are shaded blue, tan, and pink.

Topeo, 1934. Simple forms decorated with four vertical evenly spaced cascades of leaves in high relief at their origin, tapering downward to a point. A light green crystalline glaze shades to a mottled medium blue, with cascades in alternating green and pink. A second type is done completely in a high gloss dark red.

Tourist, before 1916. Glossy creamware decorated by means of a perforated wax stencil (pouncing) depicting a touring car on the way to an inn. Vases in three sizes, 8", 9", and 12" and a spittoon are shown in the catalogs; other pieces have surfaced.

Tourmaline, 1933. Although the semi-gloss medium blue, highlighted around the rim with lighter high gloss and gold effect, seems to be accepted as the standard Tourmaline glaze, the catalog definitely shows this and two other types as well. One is a mottled over-all turquoise, the other a mottled salmon which appears to be lined in the high gloss, but with no over-run to the outside.*

Tuscany, 1927. Marble-like finish most often found in a shiny pink, sometimes in matte gray, more rarely in a dull light blue. Suggestion of leaves and berries, usually at the base of handles, is the only decoration.

Velmoss, 1935. Characterized by three horizontal wavy lines around the top from which long, blade-like leaves extend downward. Colors are green, blue, or red; tan is rare.

Velmoss Scroll, 1916. Incised pattern is "cut" into ivory background; added colors are in the incised lines only, red roses, green leaves, and brown branches.

Venetian, early 1900s. Utilitarian ware; crockery type; in blue or yellow outside, lined with white.*

Victorian Art Pottery, 1924 – 28. Simple shapes, slip decorated designs. Tailored to customer preference with choice of scarabs, grapes and leaves, and sailing ships. The first two variations are illustrated in the color plates; the ship motif is rare (see Volume II).

Vista, 1920s. Tall trees with palm-like branches, each with a single fruit, line both sides of a narrow lake or canal. Color combination is generally green, blue, and gray. Though sometimes referred to as Forest, collectors prefer the Vista designation.

Volpato, 1918. Finely modeled, classic forms, fluted either at the top or the base, or not at all. Much variation in the line; some pieces show garlands of vines and small roses, sometimes caught up by a grape leaf. Tall pieces have cascades of flowers.

Water Lily, 1945. Water lily and pad in various color combinations: tan to brown with yellow lily; blue with white lily; rose to green, with pink lily.

White Rose, late 1940s. Spray of white roses and green leaves on shaded backgrounds of blue; brown to green; and pink to green.

Wincraft, 1948. Revived shapes from older lines such as Pine Cone, Bushberry, Cremona, Primrose, and others. Vases with animal motif, contemporary shapes in high gloss of blue, tan, lime, and green.

Windsor, 1931. Rust or blue mottled glaze, some with leaves, vines, and ferns; some with a repetitive band arrangement of small squares and rectangles in yellow and green.

Wisteria, 1933. Roughly textured backgrounds shading from tan to deep blue, more rarely in only tan, decorated with green vine and lavender wisteria.

Woodland, Rozane, 1905 – 06. Stippled bisque backgrounds with incised decorations of naturalistic flowers and leaves colored with glossy enamel. Also see text.

Zephyr Lily, 1946. Tall lilies and slender leaves adorn swirl-textured backgrounds of Bermuda blue, evergreen, and sienna tan.

Rozane
If marked: Rozane, RPCo; RPCo; round Rozane seal; Rozane seal with chevron.

Plate 1
Row 1:
    Bowl, 2½", #927 . . . . $100.00 – 125.00
    Bud Vase, 4", #862 . . . . $135.00 – 165.00
    Vase 4" . . . . $135.00 – 165.00
    Bowl, 2½", #927 . . . . $100.00 – 125.00
Row 2:
    Ewer, 11", #870 – 4 . . . . $400.00 – 500.00
    Commemorative Vase, 5", #923 . . . . $200.00 – 250.00
    Ewer, 7", #828 . . . . $300.00 – 350.00
    Same as above.
Row 3:
    Jug, 4½", #888 . . . . $200.00 – 225.00
    Pillow Vase, 9" #882, artist signed: F. Steele . . . . $4,000.00 – 5,000.00
    Vase, 4", #844, artist signed: F. R. . . . . $125.00 – 150.00
Row 4:
    Vase, 9½", #821 . . . . $350.00 – 400.00
    Vase, 14", artist signed: Mitchell . . . . $450.00 – 500.00
    Vase, 9½", #821 . . . . $350.00 – 400.00

Plate 1

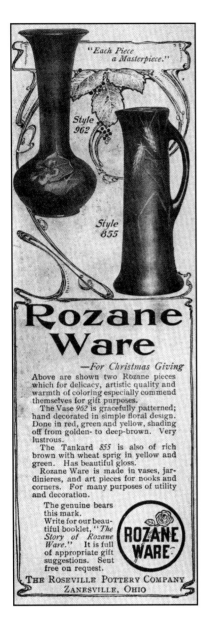

Rozane, Rozane Light

Marks: Rozane, RPCo; round Rozane seals; Rozane seal with chevron.

Plate 2

Row 1:

Vase 4" . . . . $175.00 – 200.00
Jug, 7", artist signed: J. Imlay. . . . . $250.00 – 300.00
Pitcher, 5", artist signed: Mae Timberlake . . . . $350.00 – 400.00
Paperweight, artist signed: Grace Neff . . . . $300.00 – 350.00
UNTRIMMED ROZANE Ewer, 8", no art work . . . . $175.00 – 200.00
Tobacco Jar, 6", artist signed: Walter Myers . . . . . . $500.00 – 600.00
Pitcher, 4" . . . . $150.00 – 200.00

Row 2:

Vase 6½", artist signed: Virginia Adams . . . . $400.00 – 450.00
Vase, 6", artist signed: J. Imlay . . . . $450.00 – 500.00
Vase 10", artist signed: Walter Myers . . . . $650.00 – 750.00
Pitcher, 7", with squeeze-bag decor,
    artist signed: Mary Pierce. . . . . $2,500.00 – 3,000.00
Vase, 9" . . . . $500.00 – 550.00
Vase, 8", artist signed: May Timberlake. . . . . $500.00 – 550.00

Row 3:

Tankard, 11½", artist signed: J. Imlay. . . . . $700.00 – 800.00
Vase, 14", artist signed: J. Imlay . . . . $3,000.00 – 3,500.00
Vase, 5", artist signed: Grace Neff . . . . $150.00 – 175.00
Vase, 16", artist signed: J. Imlay . . . . $3,000.00 – 3,500.00
Pillow Vase, 10 x 10",
    artist signed: Walter Myers. . . . . $1,200.00 – 1,500.00

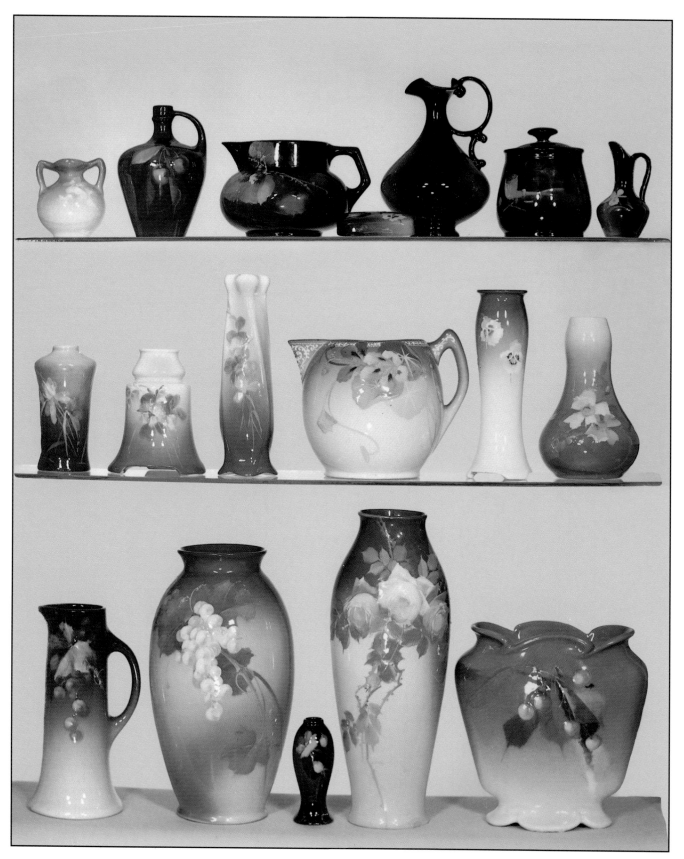

Plate 2

Azurean
Marks: RPCo or AZUREAN.

Plate 3
    Vase, 4½", artist signed: Virginia Adams. . . . . $450.00 – 550.00

Cornelian
Marks: None

Plate 4
    Cracker Jar and Lid . . . . $250.00 – 350.00

Plate 3

Plate 4

Rozane, Rozane Light
Marks: Rozane, RPCo; round Rozane seal; Rozane seal with chevron.

Plate 5
Row 1:
    Bud Vase, 8", #842 . . . . $150.00 – 175.00
    Vase, 6", #883, artist signed . . . . $200.00 – 250.00
    Vase, 9", artist signed: Pillsbury . . . . $1,200.00 – 1,500.00
    Bud Vase, 6", #831 . . . . $125.00 – 150.00
    Vase, with lid, 7½", #901 . . . . $550.00 – 650.00
Row 2:
    Mug, 4½", #886, artist signed: Harry Rhead . . . . $175.00 – 200.00
    Vase, 7" . . . . $150.00 – 175.00
    Bowl . . . . $200.00 – 250.00
    Vase, 5½", #853, artist signed . . . . $175.00 – 200.00

Plate 5

Rozane
Mark: Rozane, RPCo.

Plate 6

    Jardiniere and Pedestal, 31" overall, #524. . . . . $2,500.00 – 3,000.00

Egypto
Marks: Round Rozane seal; Rozane seal with chevron (all Egypto must have this seal).

Plate 7

    Oil Lamp, 5" . . . . $1,500.00 – 2,000.00
    Vase, 11" . . . . $1,750.00 – 2,250.00

Plate 8

    Compote, 9" . . . . $1,500.00 – 1,750.00
    Pitcher, 5" . . . . $750.00 – 1,000.00

Plate 6

Plate 7

Plate 8

Mongol

If marked: Round Rozane seal; Rozane seal with chevron.

Plate 9

Vase, 3"..$400.00 – 500.00 [1]
Vase, 10"...$3,000.00 – 3,500.00
Pitcher, 6½"...$700.00 – 800.00 [2]

Plate 10

Vase, 15"...$1,500.00 – 2,000.00

Mara

If marked: Round Rozane seal; Rozane seal with chevron.

Plate 11

Vase, 13½"..$6,000.00 – 7,500.00

Crystalis

If marked: Round Rozane seal.

Plate 12

Ewer, 7½"...$1,750.00 – 2,000.00

Note: Rozane wafers add at least 25% to the value of Mara, Mongol, and Crystalis.
[1] This is a trial glaze on a Mongol blank.
[2] The mottled glaze on this ewer indicates it was sold as a factory second. The price could triple if it had a perfect glaze.

Plate 9

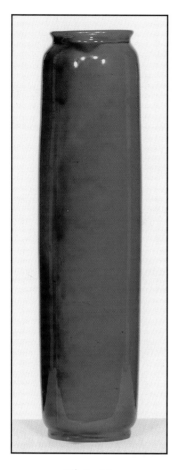

Plate 10

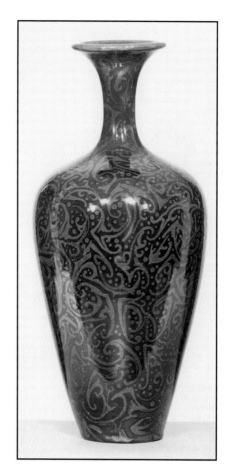

Plate 11

Plate 12

Woodland
If marked: Round Rozane seal; Rozane seal with chevron.

Plate 13

Vase, 8" . . . . $1,250.00 – 1,500.00
Vase, 10" . . . . $1,500.00 – 1,750.00
Vase, 9" . . . . $1,500.00 – 1,750.00

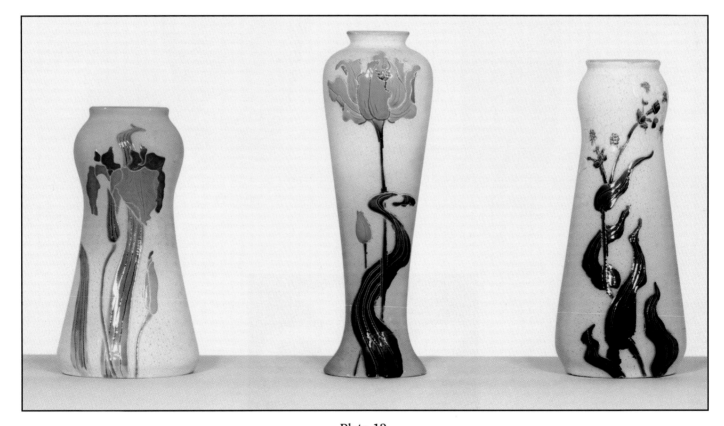

Plate 13

Fudji
If marked: Round Rozane seal; Rozane seal with chevron.

Plate 14

Vase, 9½" . . . . $2,500.00 – 3,000.00
Vase 10" . . . . $3,000.00 – 3,500.00

Note: Rozane wafers add at least 25% to the value of Fudji and Woodland.

Plate 14

Decorated Pauleo
If marked: Pauleo seal.

Plate 15

Vase, 20" . . . . $2,500.00 – 3,000.00

When we purchased this vase, with it came this interesting and enlightening letter, signed by a former employee of the Roseville Company. The girls who were working on the line at the time these vases were made each had the opportunity to buy one, and this vase had been in this lady's home since that time.

"This unusual piece of decorated Pauleo was manufactured by the Roseville Pottery Company of Zanesville, Ohio, in 1918 or 1919. Total production of these vases did not exceed over seventy-five or eighty.* They were distributed in New York City and sold for $75.00 when originally manufactured. Miss Gray was the decorator of this piece."

*This figure was no doubt accurate at the time this statement was made, but today there are at least two hundred decorated Pauleo vases accounted for.

Plate 15

Della Robbia
If marked: Round Rozane seal.

Plate 16
   Vase, 13" . . . . $5,000.00 – 6,000.00

Olympic
Mark: Rozane Olympic Pottery in black ink.

Plate 17
   Vase, 13" . . . . $4,000.00 – 5,000.00

Plate 18
   Tankard, 11", in black ink: Triptalemos and a Grain of Wheat. . . . . $2,500.00 – 3,000.00

Plate 16

Plate 17

Plate 18

Aztec
Mark: None

Plate 19
Row 1:
Pitcher, 5"..$350.00 – 400.00
Pitcher, 5½", artist signed: L...............................$350.00 – 400.00
Row 2:
Vase, 10", artist signed: M.................................$700.00 – 800.00
Lamp base, 11"..$700.00 – 800.00
Vase, 9½", artist signed: C................................$600.00 – 700.00
Vase, 8", artist signed: C.................................$500.00 – 600.00

Plate 19

Tourist
Mark: None

Plate 20
Vase, 12" . . . . $2,000.00 – 2,500.00

Matt Color
If marked: Paper or foil sticker.

Plate 21
Bowl, 4" . . . . $50.00 – 75.00
Hanging Basket, 4½" . . . . $75.00 – 95.00
Bowl, 3" . . . . $40.00 – 60.00

Matt Green
Mark: None

Plate 22
The Gate. . . . . $75.00 – 95.00

Plate 21

Plate 20

Plate 22

Dutch, Creamware
Mark: None

Plate 23

Pitcher, 9½" . . . . $250.00 – 350.00
CREAMWARE Mug, 5", decal of Biblical scene . . . . $200.00 – 250.00

Plate 24

Row 1:

Mug, 5", rare decal . . . . $150.00 – 200.00
Soap Dish, 3" . . . . $250.00 – 300.00
Tobacco Jar, 5", without lid, $150.00 – 200.00; with lid . . . . $350.00 – 400.00
Mug, 5" . . . . $75.00 – 95.00
Mug, 5" . . . . $75.00 – 95.00

Row 2:

Pitcher, 9" . . . . $400.00 – 450.00
Bowl, 12" . . . . $300.00 – 350.00
Pitcher, 11" . . . . $450.00 – 500.00 [1]
Tankard, 11½" . . . . $200.00 – 250.00

[1] This 11" pitcher belongs in the bowl on the left, rather than the smaller one shown with it.

Plate 23

Plate 24

Forget-Me-Not
Mark: Generally none.

Plate 25
Dresser Set, including hair receiver, powder jar, ring tree, and dresser tray . . $300.00 – 350.00

Decorated and Gold Traced

Plate 26
Candlestick, 9" . . . . $200.00 – 250.00

Gold Traced, before 1916

Plate 27
Candlestick, 9" . . . . $150.00 – 200.00

Plate 25

Plate 26

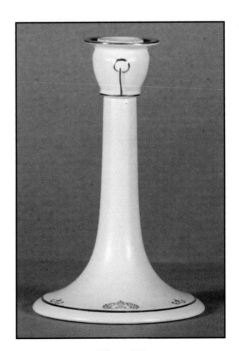

Plate 27

Creamware

Mark: Generally none.

Plate 28

Ashtray, "Drink Reyam Club Whiskey"................................$75.00 – 95.00
Quaker Mug, 5"..$200.00 – 250.00
Ashtray, "K. of P.," Grand Lodge, Zanesville, Ohio, June 8, 1915............$75.00 – 95.00

Plate 29

Mug, 5", Shrine emblem, Osman Temple, Feb. 14, 1916................$135.00 – 150.00
Tankard, 11½", Elk...$200.00 – 250.00
Mug, 6½", marked with the Rozane Ware seal, Aladdin Patrol,
        Al. G. Field, Aug. 6–06..$400.00 – 500.00
Tankard, 11½", Royal Order of Moose, "Howdy, Pap"................$175.00 – 200.00
Mug, 5", Royal Order of Moose.................................$100.00 – 125.00

Plate 28

Plate 29

Carnelian I
Marks: Large Rv ink stamp; paper sticker.

Plate 30
Row 1:
Candle Holder, 3" . . . .$50.00 – 75.00
Candle Holder, 3" . . . .$50.00 – 75.00
Vase, 6" . . . .$75.00 – 85.00
Loving Cup, 5" . . . .$100.00 – 125.00
Flower Holder, 6½" . . . .$75.00 – 85.00
Candle Holder, 2½" . . . .$30.00 – 40.00
Row 2:
Vase, 8" . . . .$150.00 – 200.00
Ewer, 15" . . . .$400.00 – 500.00
Console Bowl, 14" . . . .$150.00 – 200.00

Plate 30

Carnelian II
Marks: Large Rv ink stamp; paper sticker.

Plate 31a
Vase, 6½" . . . . $400.00 – 450.00

Plate 31b
Vase, 5" . . . . $150.00 – 200.00
Vase, 7" . . . . $250.00 – 300.00
Vase 10" . . . . $375.00 – 450.00
Vase 9" . . . . $375.00 – 450.00
Fan Vase, 8" . . . . $350.00 – 400.00

Plate 31a

Plate 31b

Mostique

If marked: Rv ink stamp; on rare occasions with an ink-stamped MOSTIQUE in a semicircular arrangement.

Plate 32

Vase, 6" . . . . $100.00 – 125.00
Vase, 10" . . . . $175.00 – 200.00
Jardiniere, 10" . . . . $300.00 – 400.00
Bowl, 2½", glossy beige exterior. . . . . $125.00 – 150.00
Vase, 6" . . . . $175.00 – 225.00

Plate 32

Imperial I
Mark: None

Plate 33
Row 1:

Basket, 6" . . . . $150.00 – 175.00
Basket, 6" . . . . $150.00 – 175.00
Vase, 8" . . . . $150.00 – 175.00
Triple Bud Vase, 8" . . . . $150.00 – 175.00
Basket, 8" . . . . $200.00 – 250.00
Basket, 6" . . . . $175.00 – 225.00
Row 2:

Basket, 11" . . . . $300.00 – 350.00
Vase, 10" . . . . $250.00 – 300.00
Lamp Base, 12" . . . . $200.00 – 250.00
Basket, 13" . . . . $350.00 – 400.00

Plate 33

Ceramic Design
Mark: None

Plate 34
Jardiniere, 4", without liner, $75.00 – 95.00; with liner . . . . $175.00 – 200.00
Wall Pocket, Persian type . . . . $500.00 – 600.00
Wall Pocket, Ceramic type . . . . $400.00 – 450.00

Roseville Dealer Signs
Mark: None

Plate 35
"Roseville Pottery" Display Sign, Moderne, "script" style, 4½" x 10" . . . . . $2,500.00 – 3,000.00
"Roseville" Display Sign, 1940s, 5" x 8" . . . . $3,000.00 – 3,500.00
"Roseville" Display Sign, 2" x 6", made for Futura line, double-sided, 1920s . . . $4,000.00 – 4,500.00

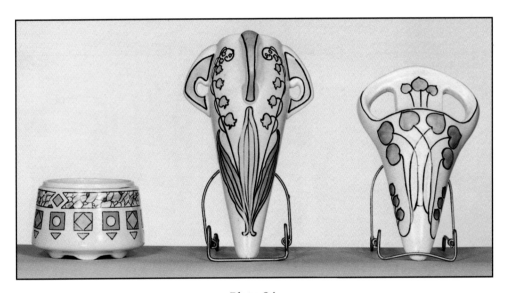

Plate 34

Plate 35

Medallion
Mark: None

Plate 36
    Dresser Set, rare color, includes tray 10", ring tree,
        hair receiver, and powder box . . . . $400.00 – 500.00

Early Pitchers
Mark: None

Plate 37
    Landscape, 7½" . . . . $175.00 – 250.00
    Tulips, 7½" . . . . $175.00 – 250.00

Plate 36

Plate 37

Landscape
Mark: None

Plate 38

    Covered Sugar, 3½" . . . . $125.00 – 150.00
    Planter, 4½" . . . . $125.00 – 150.00
    Creamer, 3" . . . . $100.00 – 125.00

Decorated Utility Ware
Mark: Large Rv ink stamp.

Plate 39

    Pitcher, 7" . . . . $150.00 – 200.00
    Pitcher, 6" . . . . $150.00 – 200.00
    Pitcher, Lily of the Valley, 7" . . . . $200.00 – 250.00
    Pitcher, Lily of the Valley, 4" . . . . $150.00 – 175.00

Plate 38

Plate 39

Rozane (1917)
If marked: Roseville Pottery Rozane ink stamp.

Plate 40
Row 1:
    Basket, 6", in pink . . . . $175.00 – 225.00
    Candlestick, 6", in ivory . . . . $100.00 – 125.00
    Spittoon, 5" in ivory, rare . . . . $250.00 – 300.00
    Compote, 5", in green . . . . $125.00 – 150.00
Row 2:
    Basket, 8", in green . . . . $250.00 – 300.00
    Basket, 11", in ivory . . . . $300.00 – 350.00
    Champagne Bucket, in ivory . . . . $300.00 – 350.00
    Vase, 7", in yellow . . . . $125.00 – 150.00

Plate 40

Juvenile
If marked: Small Rv ink stamp (may carry shape number in black or red ink).
(Matt glaze unless noted.)

Plate 42
Milk Pitcher, with chicks . . . . $175.00 – 200.00
Side-pour Creamer, with standing rabbit . . . . $175.00 – 200.00
Chamber, with chicks. with lid, $800.00 – 900.00; without lid . . . . $300.00 – 350.00
Pitcher, with saucer, both with chicks . . . . $225.00 – 250.00
Milk Pitcher, with standing rabbit . . . . $150.00 – 175.00

Plate 43
Row 1:
Mug, 3", standing rabbit . . . . $150.00 – 200.00
Bowl, (under mug), 5½" . . . . $175.00 – 200.00
Two-handled Mug, 3", high gloss, with sitting dog, rare . . . . $300.00 – 350.00
"Baby's Plate," rolled edge, 6½", with chicks . . . . $150.00 – 175.00
Oatmeal Bowl, 5½", with standing rabbit . . . . $200.00 – 225.00
Egg Cup, 3", with chick, very rare . . . . $700.00 – 800.00
Mug, 3½", with chick . . . . $200.00 – 250.00
Row 2:
Plate, 7", with chicks . . . . $200.00 – 225.00
Mug, 3", with chicks . . . . $150.00 – 200.00
Plate, 8", with standing rabbit . . . . $225.00 – 250.00
Two-handled Mug, 3", with standing rabbit, rare . . . . $300.00 – 350.00
Rolled Edge Plate, 8", high gloss, with ducks . . . . $175.00 – 200.00
Row 3:
Rolled Edge Plate 8", "Little Bo Peep" . . . . $175.00 – 200.00
Creamer, 3½", high gloss with Peter Rabbit, blue band, rare . . . . $300.00 – 350.00
Rolled Edge Plate, 8", "Tom the Piper's Son" . . . . $175.00 – 200.00
Creamer, 3½", high gloss with sunbonnet girl . . . . $150.00 – 175.00
Rolled Edge Plate, 8", "Little Jack Horner" . . . . $175.00 – 200.00

Note: All Juvenile prices are based on strong colors and transfers with little or no wear and mint condition. (Though not every piece in our photographs meets this criteria, our values reflect it.)

Plate 42

Plate 43

Velmoss Scroll*
Mark: None

Plate 44
    Jardiniere and Pedestal, 10" jardiniere, 30" overall . . . . $2,000.00 – 2,500.00

Plate 45
    Row 1:
    Candlestick, 8" . . . .$175.00 – 225.00
    Bowl, 2½" x 9" . . . .$125.00 – 150.00
    Candlestick, 9" . . . .$175.00 – 225.00
    Row 2:
    Vase, 6" . . . .$175.00 – 200.00
    Compote, 9" diameter, 4" high . . . .$200.00 – 250.00
    Candlestick, 9" . . . .$200.00 – 250.00

* The name for this line is under investigation.

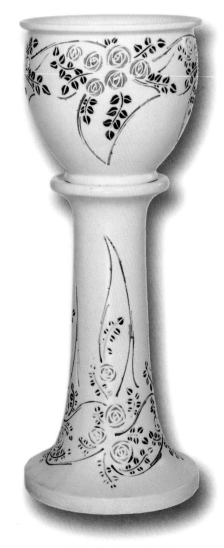

Plate 44

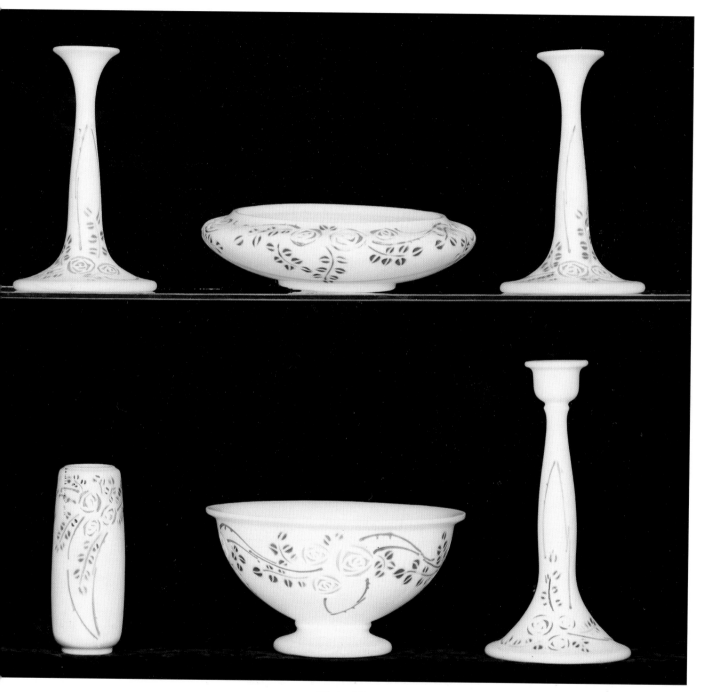

Plate 45

Rosecraft Black
If marked: Foil and paper stickers.

Plate 46
  Vase, 10", no mark . . . . $175.00 – 200.00

Rosecraft
If marked: Rv ink stamp; foil and paper stickers.

Plate 47
  Vase, 8" . . . . $100.00 – 125.00

Plate 48
  Vase 6" . . . . $100.00 – 125.00
  Bowl, 2½" . . . . $100.00 – 125.00
  Frog . . . . $15.00 – 25.00

Plate 46

Plate 47

Plate 48

Florane
Mark: Rv ink stamp.

Plate 49
Bowl, 8" diameter. . . . . $75.00 – 85.00
Vase, 6". . . . . $75.00 – 95.00
Bud Vases, 8", each. . . . . $75.00 – 95.00
Bowl Vase, 3½". . . . . $95.00 – 110.00

Persian
If marked: Roseville Pottery, Zanesville, O, in a red ink stamp.

Plate 50
Sugar and Creamer . . . . $200.00 – 250.00
Jardiniere. . . . . $350.00 – 400.00
Bowl, 3½". . . . . $175.00 – 200.00

Plate 49

Plate 50

Corinthian
If marked: Rv ink stamp.

Plate 51
Row 1:
Vase, 6" . . . . $150.00 – 175.00
Compote, 10" diameter, 5" high . . . . $150.00 – 175.00
Ashtray, 2" . . . . $175.00 – 200.00
Double Bud Vase, 7" . . . . $200.00 – 225.00
Row 2:
Candlestick, 8" . . . . $100.00 – 125.00
Vase, 8" . . . . $175.00 – 200.00
Vase, 10½" . . . . $250.00 – 300.00
Vase, 8" . . . . $150.00 – 175.00
Candlestick, 10" . . . . $125.00 – 150.00

Plate 51

Savona
If marked: Paper sticker.

Plate 52
    Vase, 10" . . . . $200.00 – 250.00

Normandy
If marked: Paper sticker.

Plate 53
    Jardiniere, 7" . . . . $250.00 – 300.00

Victorian Art Pottery
If marked: Rv ink stamp

Plate 54
    Covered Jar, 9", Grapevines, with lid, $800.00 – 900.00; without lid . . . . $500.00 – 600.00
    Vase, 10", Scarab. . . . . $800.00 – 900.00

Plate 53

Plate 52

Plate 54

Dogwood II
Mark: Rv ink stamp.

Plate 55
Row 1, two center items:

Wall Pocket . . . . $350.00 – 400.00

Vase, 6" . . . . $175.00 – 200.00

Dogwood I
Mark: None; sometimes may carry dark blue shape numbers.

Plate 55
Row 1:

Basket, 6", extreme left. . . . . $175.00 – 225.00

Bowl, 2", extreme right . . . . $75.00 – 100.00

Row 2:

Basket, 8" . . . . $200.00 – 250.00

Boat Planter, 6" . . . . $350.00 – 400.00

Double Wall Pocket . . . . $450.00 – 500.00

Bud Vase, 8" . . . . $100.00 – 125.00

Row 3:

Vase, 8" . . . . $150.00 – 175.00

Bud Vase, 9" . . . . $75.00 – 100.00

Vase, 9" . . . . $175.00 – 200.00

Vase, 12" . . . . $350.00 – 400.00

Jardiniere, 8" . . . . $300.00 – 350.00

Plate 55

Rosecraft Hexagon
Mark: Rv ink stamp.

Plate 56

Vase, 6".	Brown	$250.00 – 300.00	Green	$350.00 – 400.00
Bowl Vase, 4".	Brown	$325.00 – 375.00	Green	$450.00 – 500.00
Vase, 6".	Brown	$250.00 – 300.00	Green	$350.00 – 400.00

Plate 56

Imperial II

Rosecraft Vintage
Mark: Rv ink stamp.

Plate 57
Row 1:
    Vase, 5"...$175.00 – 200.00
    Jardiniere, 5"...$175.00 – 200.00
    Vase, 8"...$200.00 – 250.00
    Candlestick, 8"..$200.00 – 250.00
    Bowl, 6" diameter....................................$75.00 – 100.00
Row 2:
    Jardiniere, 9"...$400.00 – 450.00
    Bowl, 3½" diameter.................................$75.00 – 100.00
    Vase, 10"..$600.00 – 700.00
    Jardiniere, 8"...$350.00 – 400.00

Plate 57

Rosecraft Panel
Mark: Rv ink stamp.

Plate 58
Row 1:

Double Bud Vase	Brown	$150.00 – 175.00	Green	$200.00 – 250.00
Fan Vase, 6", with nude	Brown	$500.00 – 600.00	Green	$600.00 – 700.00
Fan Vase, 8", with nude	Brown	$700.00 – 800.00	Green	$800.00 – 900.00
Candle Holder, 2"	Brown	$60.00 – 75.00	Green	$75.00 – 100.00
Pillow Vase, 6"	Brown	$175.00 – 200.00	Green	$250.00 – 300.00

Row 2:

Candlestick, 8"	Brown	$200.00 – 250.00	Green	$300.00 – 350.00
Vase, 8"	Brown	$300.00 – 350.00	Green	$400.00 – 450.00
Vase, 9"	Brown	$350.00 – 400.00	Green	$450.00 – 500.00
With lid	Brown	$500.00 – 550.00	Green	$600.00 – 650.00
Vase, 8"	Brown	$250.00 – 275.00	Green	$350.00 – 400.00
Candlestick, 8"	Brown	$200.00 – 250.00	Green	$300.00 – 350.00

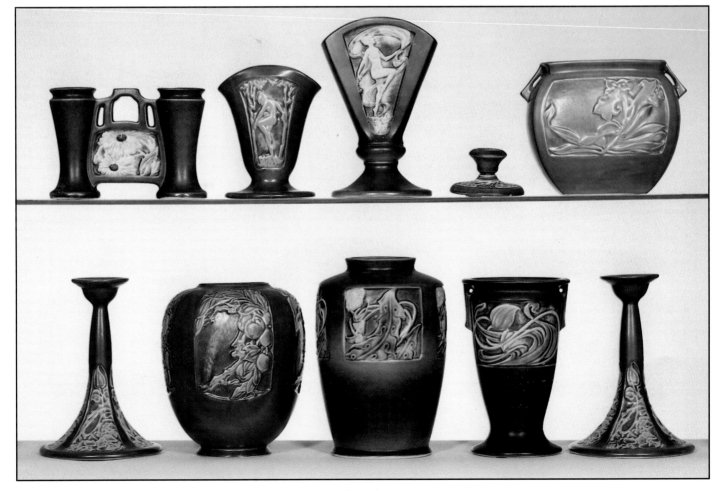

Plate 58

La Rose
Mark: Rv ink stamp.

Plate 59
Row 1:
    Bowl, 6" diameter . . . . $100.00 – 125.00
    Bowl, 9" diameter . . . . $125.00 – 150.00
    Candle Holders, 4", pair . . . . $200.00 – 225.00
Row 2:
    Double Bud Vase . . . . $150.00 – 175.00
    Vases, 10", each . . . . $250.00 – 275.00
    Double Bud Vase . . . . $150.00 – 175.00

Plate 59

Dahlrose
If marked: Paper sticker.

Plate 60
Row 1:
Triple Bud Vase, 6" . . . . $150.00 – 175.00
Vase, 6" . . . . $300.00 – 350.00
Center Bowl, oval, 10" wide . . . . $175.00 – 200.00
Double Bud Vase. . . . . $150.00 – 175.00
Row 2:
Vase, 8" . . . . $300.00 – 350.00
Vase, 10" . . . . $450.00 – 500.00
Vase, 10" . . . . $350.00 – 400.00
Vase, 10" . . . . $400.00 – 450.00
Bud Vase, 8" . . . . $350.00 – 400.00

Plate 60

Tuscany
If marked: Paper sticker.

Plate 61
Row 1:

Candle Holders, 4" pair. .	Pink . . . . . . $125.00 – 150.00	Gray/Light Blue	$100.00 – 125.00
Flower-arranger Vase, 5".	Pink . . . . . . $125.00 – 150.00	Gray/Light Blue	$100.00 – 125.00
Candle Holders, 3", pair. .	Pink . . . . . $125.00 – 150.00	Gray/Light Blue	$100.00 – 125.00

Row 2:

Vase, 8".	Pink . . . . . . $150.00 – 175.00	Gray/Light Blue	$125.00 – 150.00
Console Bowl, 11" wide. .	Pink . . . . . . $150.00 – 175.00	Gray/Light Blue	$125.00 – 150.00
Vase, 8".	Pink . . . . . . $200.00 – 225.00	Gray/Light Blue	$150.00 – 175.00

Plate 61

Imperial II
If marked: Paper sticker.

Plate 62
    Wall Pocket . . . . $700.00 – 800.00

Florentine
Mark: Rv ink stamp.

Plate 63
    Double Bud Vase, 6" . . . . $100.00 – 125.00
    Basket, 8" . . . . $200.00 – 250.00
    Compote, 10" diameter. . . . . $125.00 – 150.00
    Vase, ivory, 9" . . . . $175.00 – 200.00
    Lamp (post-factory conversion) . . . . $300.00 – 350.00
    Compote, ivory, 5" . . . . $100.00 – 125.00
    Wall Pocket, 7" . . . . $175.00 – 200.00
    Vase, 8½" . . . . $125.00 – 150.00
    Wall Pocket, 9½" . . . . $225.00 – 250.00
    Vase, 6½" . . . . $100.00 – 125.00
    Bowl, 9" diameter. . . . . $75.00 – 100.00

Lustre
If marked: Paper sticker; Rv impressed.

Plate 64
    Candle Holder, 8" . . . . $50.00 – 60.00
    Candle Holder, 10" . . . . $65.00 – 85.00
    Vase, 10" . . . . $100.00 – 125.00
    Candle Holder, 6" . . . . $45.00 – 55.00

Plate 62

Plate 63

Plate 64

Futura

If marked: Foil or paper sticker.

Plate 65

Vase, 6", #428 . . . . $550.00 – 650.00

Plate 66

Vase, 8", #401 . . . . $500.00 – 600.00

Vase, 8", #404 . . . Blue . . . . . . $2,000.00 – 2,500.00   Green . . . . $1,500.00 – 2,000.00

Cremona

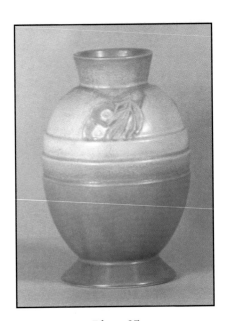

Plate 65

Plate 66

Plate 67

Row 1:
Bud Vase, 6", #422 . . . . $400.00 – 450.00
Candle Holder, 4", pair, #1073 . . . . $500.00 – 550.00
Planter, 7" wide, #191 . . . . $500.00 – 600.00
Vase, 6", #381 . . . . $400.00 – 450.00
Row 2:
Vase, 8", #385 . . . . $500.00 – 600.00
Bud Vase, 10", #390 . . . Brown . . . . $800.00 – 900.00   Blue . . . . $1,200.00 – 1,300.00
Vase, 10", #395 . . . . $1,250.00 – 1,500.00
Vase, 10", #408 . . . . $2,000.00 – 2,500.00
Vase, 8", #426 . . . . $2,000.00 – 2,500.00

Plate 67

Cremona, 1927
If marked: Paper sticker.

Plate 68
Vase, 10" . . . . $350.00 – 400.00

Plate 69
Row 1:
Candle Holder, 4" . . . . $75.00 – 85.00
Vase, 7" . . . . $100.00 – 125.00
Candle Holder, 4" . . . . $75.00 – 85.00
Row 2:
Vase, 10½" . . . . $250.00 – 300.00
Frog . . . . $50.00 – 75.00
Bowl, 9" wide . . . . $125.00 – 150.00
Vase, 8" . . . . $150.00 – 175.00

Ferella

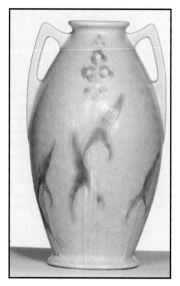

Plate 68

Plate 69

Artcraft
If marked: Foil sticker.

Plate 70, left
    Jardiniere, 6" . . . . $450.00 – 500.00

Earlam
If marked: Paper sticker.

Plate 70, right
    Vase, 7", #521-7 . . . . $375.00 – 425.00

Ixia
Mark: Roseville impressed; foil sticker.

Plate 71
Row 1:
    Basket, 10", #346 . . . . $300.00 – 350.00
    Vase, 6", #853 . . . . $150.00 – 175.00
Row 2:
    Rose Bowl, 4", #326 . . . . $150.00 – 175.00
    Bowl, 6", #327 . . . . $150.00 – 175.00

Plate 70

Plate 71

Clemana
Mark: Roseville impressed.

Plate 72
Row 1:
Vase, 7", #123 . . . . Blue . . . . $350.00 – 400.00   Green . . . $300.00 – 350.00
Tan . . . . . $250.00 – 300.00
Row 2:
Candle Holders, 4½", pair, #1104. . Blue . . . . $325.00 – 375.00   Green . . . $300.00 – 325.00
Tan . . . . . $275.00 – 325.00

Sunflower
If marked: Paper sticker.

Plate 73
Row 1:
Vase, 5½", #488 . . . . $1,100.00 – 1,300.00
Vase, 8", #491 . . . . $1,700.00 – 1,900.00
Vase, 7", #487 . . . . $1,000.00 – 1,200.00
Vase, 6", #485 . . . . $650.00 – 750.00
Row 2:
Vase, 10", #493 . . . . $1,500.00 – 1,700.00
Jardiniere, 9", #619. . . . . $2,000.00 – 2,500.00
Vase, 8", #490 . . . . $1,500.00 – 1,700.00

Plate 72

Plate 73

Thorn Apple
Mark: Roseville impressed.

Plate 74
Row 1:
    Cornucopia Vase, 6", #127 . . . . $150.00 – 175.00
    Planter, 5", #262 . . . . $150.00 – 175.00
    Vase, 6", #812 . . . . $150.00 – 175.00
Row 2:
    Candle Holder, 2½", pair, #1117 . . . . $200.00 – 225.00
    Candle Holder, 5½", pair, #1118 . . . . $300.00 – 350.00
Row 3:
    Vase, 4", #808 . . . . $150.00 – 175.00
    Basket, 10", #342 . . . . $350.00 – 400.00
    Vase, 4", #808 . . . . $150.00 – 175.00

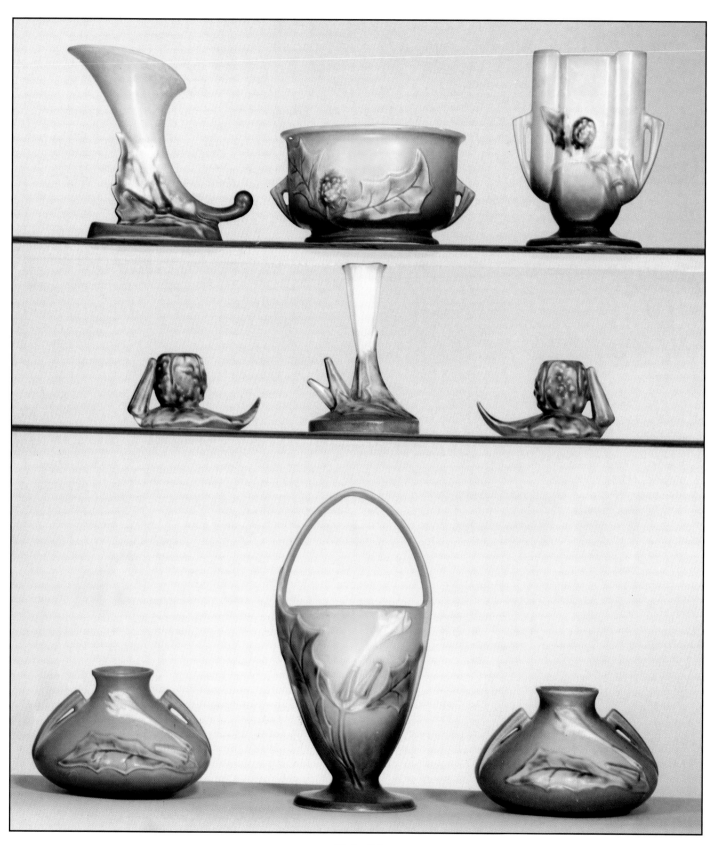

Plate 74

Iris
Mark: Roseville impressed or in relief.

Plate 75
Row 1:
    Bowl, 6", #360 . . . . Blue . . . . $200.00 – 250.00   Pink or Tan . . $175.00 – 225.00
    Wall Shelf, 8", #2 . . . . Blue . . . . $500.00 – 550.00   Pink or Tan . . $450.00 – 500.00
    Jardiniere, 5", #647 . . . . Blue . . . . $200.00 – 250.00   Pink or Tan . . $175.00 – 225.00
Row 2:
    Vase, 4", #914. . . . . Blue . . . . $125.00 – 150.00   Pink or Tan . . $100.00 – 125.00
    Center Bowl, 14", #364 . . . . . . Blue . . . . $300.00 – 350.00   Pink or Tan . . $250.00 – 300.00
    Candle Holders, 4", pair, #1135 Blue . . . . $300.00 – 350.00   Pink or Tan . . $250.00 – 300.00
Row 3:
    Ewer, 10", #926 . . . . Blue . . . . $350.00 – 400.00   Pink or Tan . . $250.00 – 300.00
    Basket, 8", #354 . . . . Blue . . . . $400.00 – 450.00   Pink or Tan . . $350.00 – 400.00

Plate 75

Poppy
Mark: Roseville impressed.

Plate 76
Row 1:
    Wall Pocket Candle Holder, 9", #1281 . . . . Pink* . . . . $900.00 – 1,000.00
                                         Gray or Green . . . . $800.00 – 900.00
    Vase, 6½", #867 . . . . Pink* . . . . $175.00 – 200.00
                                           Gray or Green . . . . $125.00 – 150.00
Row 2:
    Ewer, 10", #876. . . . . Pink* . . . . $450.00 – 550.00
                                           Gray or Green . . . . $375.00 – 450.00
    Basket, 10", #347 . . . . Pink* . . . . $450.00 – 550.00
                                           Gray or Green . . . . $375.00 – 450.00

*Tan is rare, add 50% to Pink values to price this color.

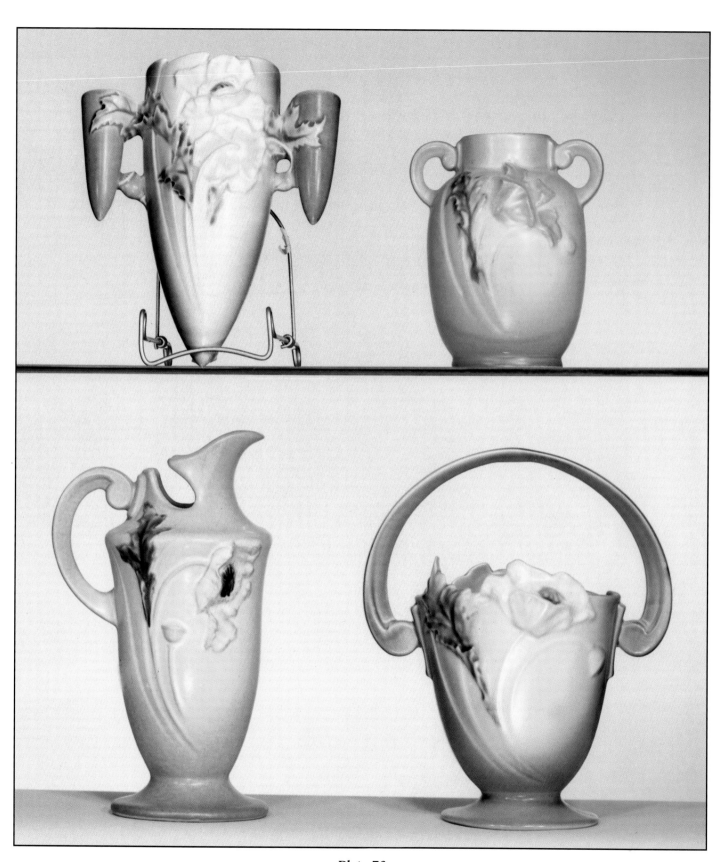

Plate 76

Moss
Mark: Roseville impressed.

Plate 77
Row 1:
Candlesticks, 4½", pair, #1107 Pink & Green or Orange & Green . . . . $275.00 – 325.00
Blue . . . . $200.00 – 225.00
Row 2:
Vase, 6", #774 . . . . Pink & Green or Orange & Green . . . . $225.00 – 250.00
Blue . . . . $175.00 – 200.00
Vase, 8", #779 . . . . Pink & Green or Orange & Green . . . . $450.00 – 500.00
Blue . . . . $375.00 – 425.00
Row 3:
Center Bowl, 12", #294 . . . . . Pink & Green or Orange & Green . . . . $300.00 – 350.00
Blue . . . . $225.00 – 250.00

Plate 77

Montacello
If marked: Paper sticker.

Plate 82
Row 1:

Vase, 4", #555. . . . . Blue . . . . $375.00 – 425.00

Tan . . . . $350.00 – 375.00

Basket, 6½", #333 . . . . Blue . . . . $1,200.00 – 1,400.00

Tan . . . . $900.00 – 1,000.00

Vase, 4", #555. . . . . Blue . . . . $375.00 – 425.00

Tan . . . . $350.00 – 375.00

Row 2:

Vase, extreme right and left, 6", #560, each . . Blue . . . . $600.00 – 700.00

Tan . . . . $500.00 – 600.00

Vase, 7", #561. . . . . Blue . . . . $750.00 – 850.00

Tan . . . . $600.00 – 700.00

Row 3:

Vase, extreme right and left, 7", #561, each . . Blue . . . . $750.00 – 850.00

Tan . . . . $600.00 – 700.00

Vase, 9", #564. . . . . Blue . . . . $1,300.00 – 1,500.00

Tan . . . . $900.00 – 1,100.00

Plate 82

Windsor
If marked: Paper or foil sticker.

Plate 83

Row 1:
Candlesticks, extreme right and left, 4½", pair, #1084
| | Blue. . . $550.00 – 650.00 | Tan. . . . . $450.00 – 550.00 |
Vase, 5", #545. . . . . Blue. . . $450.00 – 500.00 Tan. . . . . $400.00 – 450.00

Row 2:
Vase, 5", #545. . . . . Blue. . . $450.00 – 500.00 Tan. . . . . $400.00 – 450.00
Center Bowl, 16" wide, #224 . . Blue. . . $500.00 – 600.00 Tan. . . . . $400.00 – 500.00
Frog. . . . . Blue. . . . . $50.00 – 75.00 Tan. . . . . $50.00 – 75.00

Row 3:
Vase, 7", #549. . . . . Blue $1,100.00 – 1,300.00 Tan . . . . $900.00 – 1,100.00
Vase, 9" #582 . . . . Blue $1,500.00 – 1,750.00 Tan . . . . $1,000.00 – 1,250.00
Vase, 7", #549. . . . . Blue $1,100.00 – 1,300.00 Tan . . . . $900.00 – 1,100.00

Plate 83

Cosmos

Mark: Roseville impressed or in relief.

Plate 84

Row 1:

Vase, 4", #944

    Blue . . . . $150.00 – 175.00   Green . . $125.00 – 150.00   Tan . . . . 100.00 – 125.00

Bowl Vase, 6", #376

    Blue . . . . $375.00 – 425.00   Green . . $325.00 – 375.00   Tan . . . $250.00 – 300.00

Vase, 3", #649

    Blue . . . . $150.00 – 175.00   Green . . $125.00 – 150.00   Tan . . . $100.00 – 125.00

Row 2:

Basket, 12", #358

    Blue . . . . $500.00 – 550.00   Green . . $450.00 – 500.00   Tan . . . $400.00 – 450.00

Candle Holder, 4½", pair, #1137

    Blue . . . . $275.00 – 300.00   Green . . $250.00 – 275.00   Tan . . . $225.00 – 250.00

Ewer, 15", #957

    Blue . . . . . . $1,100.00 – 1,200.00   Green $1,000.00 – 1,100.00   Tan . . $900.00 – 1,000.00

Plate 84

Jonquil
If marked: Foil or paper sticker.

Plate 85
Row 1:
      Vase, 4", #539 . . . . $175.00 – 225.00
      Basket, 9", #324 . . . . $600.00 – 700.00
      Bud Vase, 7", #102 . . . . $350.00 – 400.00
      Bowl, 4", #538 . . . . $200.00 – 250.00
Row 2:
      Vase, 8", #527 . . . . $400.00 – 450.00
      Basket, 10", #328 . . . . $800.00 – 900.00
      Jardiniere, 6", #621 . . . . $300.00 – 350.00

Plate 85

Blackberry
Mark: Foil or paper stickers.

Plate 86
Row 1:
      Vase, 5", #569 . . . . $500.00 – 600.00
      Vase, 4", #567 . . . . $450.00 – 500.00
      Vase, 6", #572 . . . . $650.00 – 700.00
      Wall Pocket, #1267 . . . . $2,000.00 – 2,500.00
      Bowl, 6" wide, #226 . . . . $450.00 – 500.00
Row 2:
      Vase, 6", #574 . . . . $700.00 – 800.00
      Jardiniere, 6", #623 . . . . $550.00 – 650.00
      Vase, 6", #573 . . . . $650.00 – 700.00
      Vase, 5", #570 . . . . $500.00 – 600.00
Row 3:
      Candle Holders, 4½", pair, #1086 . . . . $700.00 – 800.00
      Center Bowl, 13" wide, #228 . . . . $700.00 – 800.00
      Vase, 4", #568 . . . . $500.00 – 550.00
Row 4:
      Vase, 8", #576 . . . . $850.00 – 950.00
      Vase, 10", #577 . . . . $1,500.00 – 1,750.00
      Vase, 12½", #578 . . . . $2,000.00 – 2,500.00
      Vase, 8", #575 . . . . $750.00 – 850.00

Plate 86

Cherry Blossom
If marked: Foil sticker.

Plate 87
Row 1:
    Candle Holders, 4", pair, #1090 Brown . . . $500.00 – 550.00   Pink & Blue . . . $750.00 – 850.00
    Bowl Vase, 6", #621. . . . . Brown . . . $450.00 – 500.00   Pink & Blue, . . . $650.00 – 750.00
    Jardiniere, 5", #627. . . . . Brown . . . $325.00 – 375.00   Pink & Blue . . . $475.00 – 525.00
Row 2:
    Vase, 5", #619 . . . . Brown . . . $350.00 – 400.00   Pink & Blue . . . $550.00 – 600.00
    Vase, 7½", #620. . . . . Brown . . . $375.00 – 425.00   Pink & Blue . . . $550.00 – 600.00
    Vase, 10", #626 . . . . Brown . . . $650.00 – 750.00   Pink & Blue. $1,100.00 – 1,200.00
    Vase, 7", #622 . . . . Brown . . . $450.00 – 500.00   Pink & Blue . . . $650.00 – 750.00
Row 3:
    Vase, 5", #619 . . . . Brown . . . $350.00 – 400.00   Pink & Blue . . . $550.00 – 600.00
    Vase, 7", #623 . . . . Brown . . . $500.00 – 550.00   Pink & Blue . . . $750.00 – 850.00
    Vase, 8", #624 . . . . Brown . . . $550.00 – 600.00   Pink & Blue . . $900.00 – 1,000.00
    Vase, 7", #622 . . . . Brown . . . $500.00 – 550.00   Pink & Blue . . . $750.00 – 850.00
    Vase, 4", #617 . . . . Brown . . . $325.00 – 375.00   Pink & Blue . . . $500.00 – 550.00
Row 4:
    Factory Lamp Base . . . . Brown. $1,250.00 – 1,500.00   Pink & Blue. $2,000.00 – 2,500.00
    Jardiniere, 10", #627. . . . . Brown. $1,250.00 – 1,500.00   Pink & Blue. . 2,000.00 – 2,500.00
    Vase, 8", #625 . . . . Brown . . . $650.00 – 750.00   Pink & Blue. $1,100.00 – 1,200.00

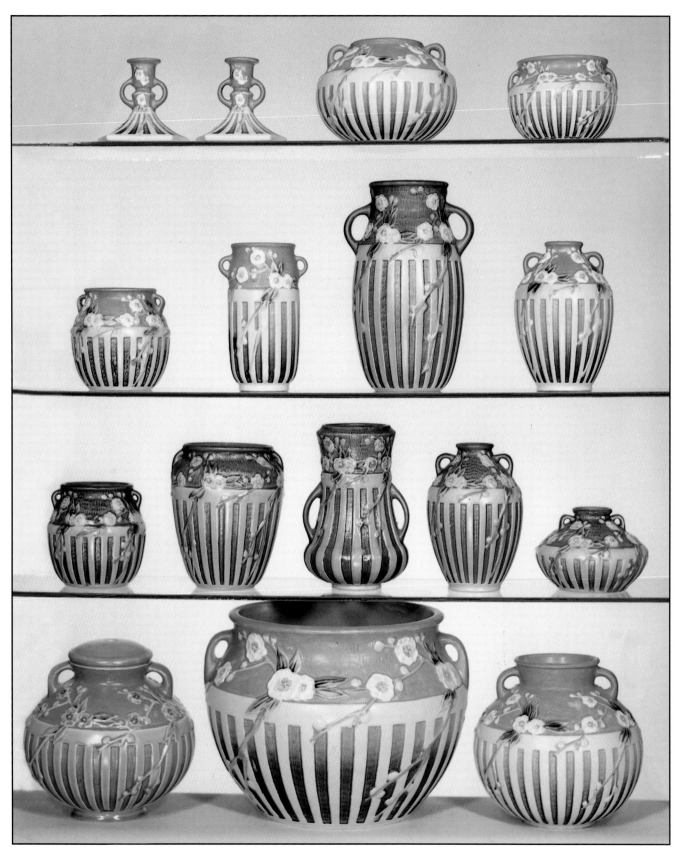

Plate 87

Baneda
If marked: Foil sticker.

Plate 88
Row 1:
      Vase, 5½", #601 . . . . Pink . . . $450.00 – 500.00   Green . . . . . . $600.00 – 650.00
      Candle Holder, 4½", #1088, pair . Pink . . . $650.00 – 750.00   Green . . . . . . $850.00 – 950.00
      Center Bowl, 13" across, #237 . . . Pink . . . $750.00 – 900.00   Green . . . . . $900.00 – 1,100.00
      Vase, 6", #588 . . . . Pink . . . $500.00 – 550.00   Green . . . . . . $600.00 – 650.00
Row 2:
      Vase, 8", #593 . . . . Pink . . . $700.00 – 800.00   Green . . . . . $900.00 – 1,000.00
      Jardiniere, 9½", #626 . . . . Pink. $1,800.00 – 2,000.00   Green . . . $2,500.00 – 2,750.00
      Vase, 8", #593 . . . . Pink . . . $700.00 – 800.00   Green . . . . . $900.00 – 1,000.00

Plate 88

Wisteria
If marked: Foil sticker.

Plate 89

Row 1:

Center Bowl, 12", #423 . . .	Tan . . . . $500.00 – 550.00	Blue . . . . . . $850.00 – 950.00
Vase, 7", #634.	Tan . . . . $550.00 – 600.00	Blue . . . . . . $850.00 – 950.00
Vase, 6", #631.	Tan . . . . $400.00 – 450.00	Blue . . . . . . $600.00 – 650.00
Bowl, 4", #242	Tan . . . . $350.00 – 400.00	Blue . . . . . . $500.00 – 550.00

Row 2:

Vase, 8", #633.	Tan . . . . $650.00 – 700.00	Blue . . . . . . $900.00 – 1,000.00
Vase, 9", #681.	Tan. . . . . . . $900.00 – 1,000.00	Blue . . . . $1,500.00 – 1,750.00
Vase, 10", #639.	Tan. . . . . . . $900.00 – 1,000.00	Blue . . . . $1,500.00 – 1,750.00
Vase, 6", #637.	Tan . . . . $800.00 – 900.00	Blue . . . . $1,400.00 – 1,600.00

Plate 89

Laurel
If marked: Foil sticker.

Plate 90

Row 1:
Bowl, 7" wide, #251 . .	Gold . . $250.00 – 275.00	Russet . $275.00 – 300.00	Green . $300.00 – 325.00
Vase, 7", #670	Gold . . $325.00 – 350.00	Russet . $350.00 – 375.00	Green . $400.00 – 450.00
Vase, 6½", #669	Gold . . $300.00 – 325.00	Russet . $325.00 – 350.00	Green . $375.00 – 425.00
Vase, 6", #667	Gold . . $275.00 – 300.00	Russet . $300.00 – 325.00	Green . $350.00 – 375.00

Row 2:
Vase, 8", #671	Gold . . $350.00 – 375.00	Russet . $400.00 – 450.00	Green . $450.00 – 500.00
Vase, 9", #675	Gold . . $550.00 – 600.00	Russet . $600.00 – 700.00	Green . $700.00 – 800.00
Vase, 8½", #672	Gold . . $500.00 – 550.00	Russet . $550.00 – 650.00	Green . $650.00 – 750.00
Vase, 6", #668	Gold . . $250.00 – 275.00	Russet . $275.00 – 300.00	Green . $300.00 – 325.00

Plate 90

Luffa
If marked: Foil sticker.

Plate 91

Jardiniere, 4", #631 . . . . $400.00 – 450.00
Vase, 7", #685 . . . . $550.00 – 650.00
Vase, 12", #691 . . . . $1,000.00 – 1,200.00
Vase, 7", #685 . . . . $550.00 – 650.00
Vase, 6", #684 . . . . $450.00 – 550.00

Plate 91

Primrose

Mark: Roseville impressed.

Plate 92

Vase, 8", #767	Blue or Pink	$350.00 – 400.00	Tan	$275.00 – 325.00
Bowl, 4", #284	Blue or Pink	$250.00 – 275.00	Tan	$200.00 – 225.00
Vase, 8", #765	Blue or Pink	$325.00 – 375.00	Tan	$250.00 – 275.00

Topeo

If marked: Foil sticker.

Plate 93

Vase, 9½", #662	Blue	$450.00 – 500.00	Red	$275.00 – 325.00

Note: Some feel the Red-Glazed Topeo should be properly identified as Mowa. Nothing in our research can either confirm or disprove this.

Plate 94

Vase, 7", #658	Blue	$400.00 – 450.00	Red	$225.00 – 275.00
Vase, 9", #661	Blue	$600.00 – 700.00	Red	$400.00 – 500.00

Plate 95

Row 1:

Bowl, 2½"	Blue	$225.00 – 250.00	Red	$150.00 – 175.00

Row 2:

Vase, 6", #245	Blue	$450.00 – 550.00	Red	$300.00 – 325.00
Vase, 6½", #656	Blue	$400.00 – 450.00	Red	$175.00 – 200.00

Plate 92

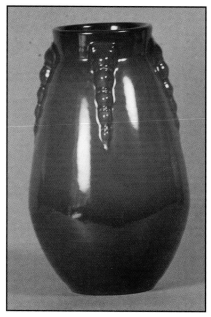

Plate 93

Plate 94

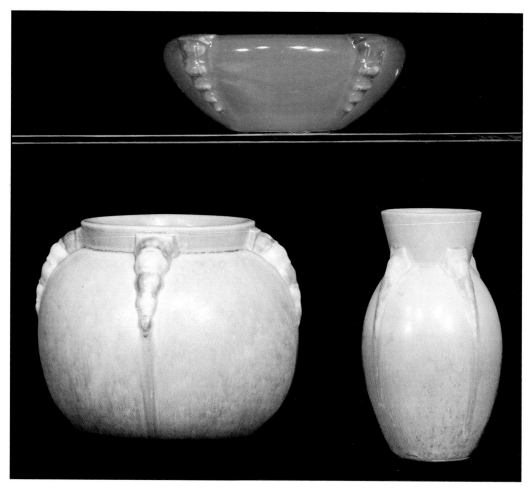

Plate 95

Pine Cone

Marks: Roseville impressed or in relief; paper sticker or Pine Cone impressed.

Plate 96
Row 1:
Triple Candle Holders,
5½", pair, #1106 . . . . Green . . . . $500.00 – 600.00   Brown. . . . $700.00 – 800.00
Blue . . . . $900.00 – 1,000.00
Bowl, 3", #632 . . . . Green . . . . $125.00 – 150.00   Brown. . . . $150.00 – 175.00
Blue . . . . . $175.00 – 225.00
Basket/Planter, 3½", #468 . . . . Green . . . . $350.00 – 400.00   Brown. . . . $475.00 – 525.00
Blue . . . . . $675.00 – 750.00
Planter, 6", #456 . . . . Green . . . . $200.00 – 250.00   Brown. . . . $250.00 – 300.00
Blue . . . . . $300.00 – 350.00
Basket, 6", #408 . . . . Green . . . . $350.00 – 400.00   Brown. . . . $450.00 – 500.00
Blue . . . . . $650.00 – 750.00
Row 2:
Fan Vase, 6", #472 . . . . Green . . . . $350.00 – 400.00   Brown. . . . $450.00 – 500.00
Blue . . . . . $650.00 – 750.00
Center Bowl, 15" wide, #323 . . . . Green . . . . $350.00 – 400.00   Brown. . . . $450.00 – 500.00
Blue . . . . . $650.00 – 750.00
Cornucopia, 8", #128 . . . . Green . . . . $200.00 – 250.00   Brown. . . . $250.00 – 300.00
Blue . . . . . $400.00 – 450.00
Row 3:
Ice-lip Pitcher, 8", #1321 . . . . Green . . . . $375.00 – 450.00   Brown. . . . $550.00 – 600.00
Blue . . . . $900.00 – 1,000.00
Cornucopia, 6", #126 . . . . Green . . . . $175.00 – 225.00   Brown. . . . $225.00 – 275.00
Blue . . . . . $350.00 – 400.00
Basket, 10", #410 . . . . Green . . . . $425.00 – 475.00   Brown. . . . $500.00 – 550.00
Blue . . . . $950.00 – 1,100.00
Pitcher, 9", #425 . . . . Green . . . . $550.00 – 650.00   Brown. . . . $750.00 – 850.00
Blue . . $1,000.00 – 1,250.00
Row 4:
Vase, 10", #709 . . . . Green . . . . $375.00 – 425.00   Brown. . . . $450.00 – 500.00
Blue . . . . . $800.00 – 900.00
Basket, 9" x 13", #339 . . . . Green . . . . $500.00 – 600.00   Brown. . . . $650.00 – 750.00
Blue . . $1,100.00 – 1,300.00
Vase, 7", #112 . . . . Green . . . . $175.00 – 200.00   Brown. . . . $250.00 – 275.00
Blue . . . . . $400.00 – 450.00
Basket, 10", #338 . . . . Green . . . . $400.00 – 450.00   Brown. . . . $500.00 – 550.00
Blue . . . . . $850.00 – 950.00

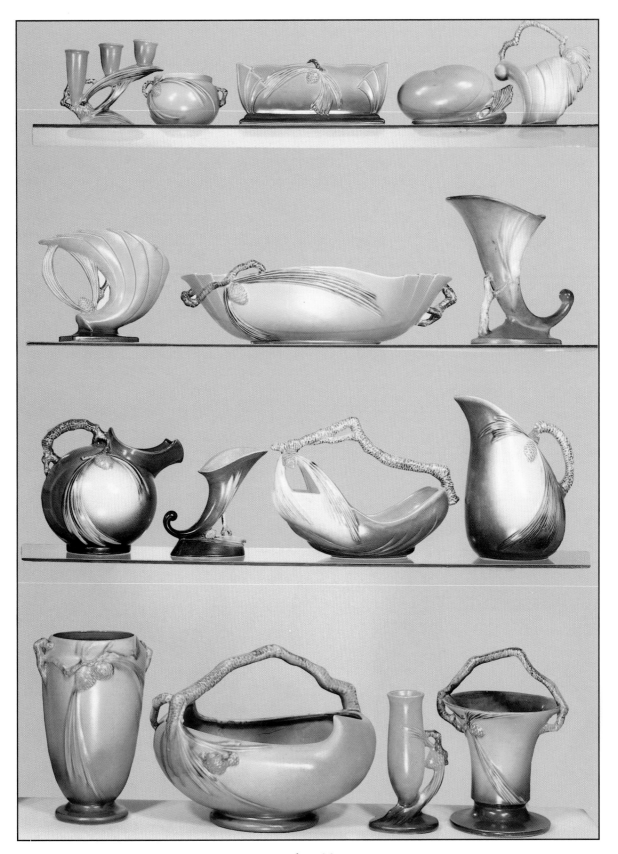

Plate 96

Velmoss

If marked: Foil sticker.

Plate 97

Vase, 7", #716	Green . . . $200.00 – 250.00	Blue . . . . $300.00 – 350.00
	Red . . . . . $350.00 – 400.00	Tan (rare) . . . . $400.00 – 450.00
Double Bud Vase, 8", #116 . .	Green . . . $200.00 – 250.00	Blue . . . . $300.00 – 350.00
	Red . . . . . $350.00 – 400.00	Tan (rare) . . . . $400.00 – 450.00
Vase, 6", #714	Green . . . $150.00 – 200.00	Blue . . . . $275.00 – 325.00
	Red . . . . . $325.00 – 375.00	Tan (rare) . . . . $375.00 – 425.00

Plate 98

Double Cornucopia, 8½", #117

Green . . . . $200.00 – 250.00	Blue . . . . $375.00 – 425.00
Red . . . . $425.00 – 475.00	Tan (rare) . . . . $475.00 – 525.00

Russco

If marked: Foil sticker.

Plate 99

Bud Vase, 8", #695 . . . . $175.00 – 200.00
Vase, 6", heavy crystals, #259 . . . . $300.00 – 350.00

Plate 100

Vase, 15", #703 . . . . $250.00 – 300.00
Vase, 6½", #259 . . . . $125.00 – 150.00

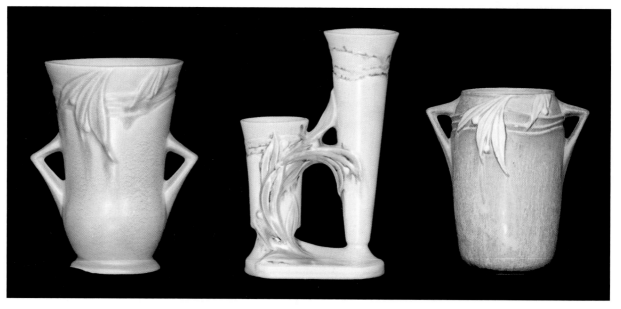

Plate 97

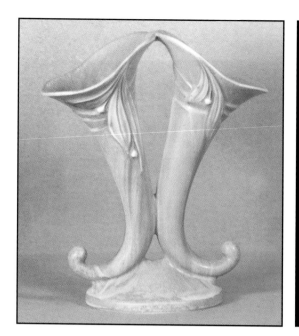

Plate 98

Plate 99

Plate 100

Morning Glory
If marked: Foil sticker.

Plate 103
Row 1:

Bowl Vase, 4", #268	Green	$450.00 – 500.00	Ivory	$350.00 – 400.00
Vase, 6", #269	Green	$800.00 – 900.00	Ivory	$500.00 – 600.00
Vase, 7", #725	Green	$650.00 – 750.00	Ivory	$450.00 – 500.00
Vase, 6", #724	Green	$450.00 – 500.00	Ivory	$350.00 – 400.00

Row 2:

Vase, 8", #727	Green	$750.00 – 850.00	Ivory	$550.00 – 600.00
Vase, 12", #731	Green	$1,750.00 – 2,000.00	Ivory	$1,000.00 – 1,100.00
Vase, 10", #730	Green	$950.00 – 1,150.00	Ivory	$650.00 – 700.00

Plate 103

Moderne
Mark: Roseville impressed or foil sticker.

Plate 104

Lamp (vase conversion), 9", #799 . . . . $400.00 – 450.00
Vase only, 9", #799 . . . . $750.00 – 850.00
Vase, 7", #794 . . . . $175.00 – 200.00

Dawn
Mark: Roseville impressed.

Plate 105

Vase, 6", #827 . . . Pink or Yellow . . . $200.00 – 250.00   Green . . . . $175.00 – 200.00
Vase, 8", #828 . . . Pink or Yellow . . . $300.00 – 350.00   Green . . . . $250.00 – 275.00
Vase, 6", #826 . . . Pink or Yellow . . . $200.00 – 250.00   Green . . . . $175.00 – 200.00

Plate 104

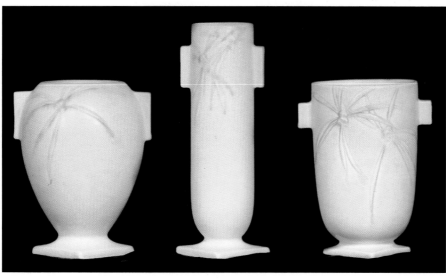

Plate 105

Rozane Pattern
Mark: Roseville in relief.

Plate 106
Bud Vase, 6", #2 . . . . $125.00 – 150.00
Planter, 14" wide, #397 . . . . $150.00 – 175.00
Vase, 6", #398 . . . . $150.00 – 175.00

Fuchsia
Mark: Roseville impressed or in relief.

Plate 107
Row 1:
Ice-lip Pitcher, 8", #1322 . . Blue . . . . $750.00 – 850.00   Green . . . . . . $550.00 – 625.00
                              Tan . . . . $475.00 – 525.00
Row 2:
Bowl Vase, 4", #346 . . . . . . Blue . . . . $200.00 – 225.00   Green . . . . . . $175.00 – 200.00
                              Tan . . . . $150.00 – 175.00
Jardiniere, 3", #645 . . . . . . Blue . . . . $150.00 – 175.00   Green . . . . . . $125.00 – 150.00
                              Tan . . . . $100.00 – 125.00
Row 3:
Vase, 7", #895 . . . . Blue . . . . $350.00 – 400.00   Green . . . . . . $300.00 – 350.00
                              Tan . . . . $250.00 – 300.00
Vase, 12", #903 . . . . Blue . . . . $850.00 – 950.00   Green . . . . . . $650.00 – 750.00
                              Tan . . . . $550.00 – 650.00
Basket and Frog, 8", #350   Blue . . . . $700.00 – 800.00   Green . . . . . . $550.00 – 600.00
                              Tan . . . . $500.00 – 550.00

Plate 106

Plate 107

Ivory II
Mark: Roseville impressed or in relief; foil sticker.

Plate 108
> Vase, 10", Carnelian shape . . . . $75.00 – 95.00

Plate 109
> Vase, 6", Savona shape, #259 . . . . $75.00 – 95.00

Plate 110
Row 1:
> Bowl Vase, 6", Russco shape, #259 . . . . $75.00 – 95.00

Row 2:
> Candelabrum, 5½" high, Velmoss shape, #1116 . . . . $175.00 – 225.00
> Bowl, 6" diameter, Matt Color shape, #550 . . . . $40.00 – 50.00

Bleeding Heart
Mark: Roseville in relief.

Plate 111
Row 1:
Vase, 4", #138	Blue	$125.00 – 150.00	Pink or Green.	$100.00 – 125.00
Wall Pocket, 8", #1287 . .	Blue	$600.00 – 650.00	Pink or Green.	$500.00 – 550.00
Pitcher, #1323	Blue	$550.00 – 600.00	Pink or Green.	$450.00 – 500.00
Ewer, 6", #963	Blue	$275.00 – 300.00	Pink or Green.	$250.00 – 275.00

Row 2:
Basket, 10", # 360	Blue	$375.00 – 425.00	Pink or Green.	$325.00 – 375.00
Basket 12", #361	Blue	$550.00 – 600.00	Pink or Green.	$450.00 – 500.00
Ewer, 10", #972	Blue	$650.00 – 750.00	Pink or Green.	$550.00 – 600.00

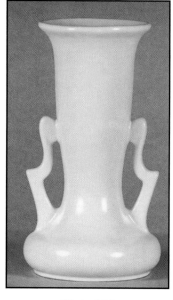

Plate 108

Plate 109

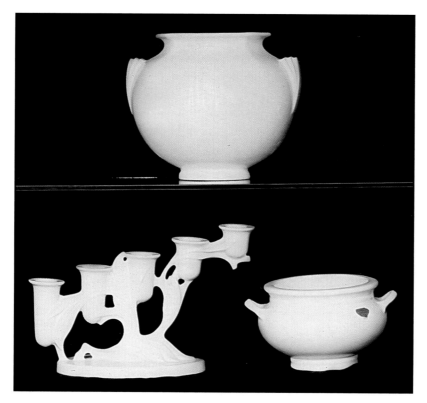

Plate 110

Plate 111

Gardenia
Mark: Roseville in relief.

Plate 112
Row 1:
    Jardiniere, 4", #600 . . . . $90.00 – 110.00
Row 2:
    Cornucopia, 6", #621 . . . . $100.00 – 125.00
    Basket, 8", #608 . . . . $225.00 – 275.00
    Ewer, 6", #616 . . . . $125.00 – 150.00
Row 3:
    Ewer, 10", #617 . . . . $250.00 – 300.00
    Basket, 10", #609 . . . . $300.00 – 350.00
    Double Cornucopia, 8", #622 . . . . $150.00 – 175.00

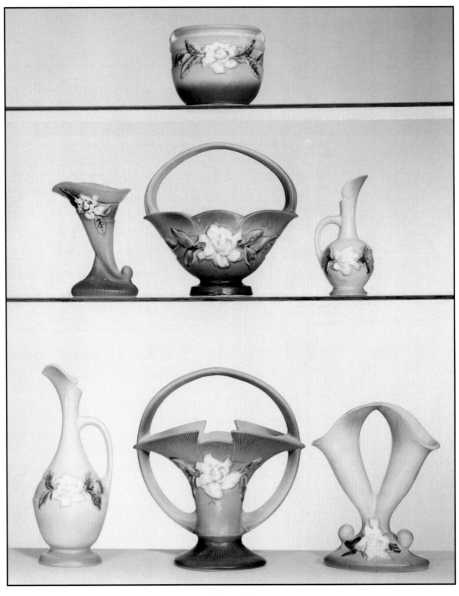

Plate 112

Bittersweet
Mark: Roseville in relief.

Plate 113

Row 1:
Double Bud Vase, 6", #873 . . . . $125.00 – 150.00
Basket, 10", #810 . . . . $250.00 – 300.00
Vase, 5", #972 . . . . $100.00 – 125.00

Row 2:
Planter, 8" wide, #868 . . . . $100.00 – 125.00
Tea set . . . . $450.00 – 550.00
Teapot, #871P
Sugar, #871S
Creamer, #871C

Row 3:
Basket, 6", #808 . . . . $175.00 – 225.00
Basket, 8", #809 . . . . $200.00 – 250.00
Vase, 8", #883 . . . . $150.00 – 175.00
Cornucopia, 8", #822 . . . . $125.00 – 150.00
Ewer, 8", #816 . . . . $250.00 – 300.00

Plate 113

White Rose
Mark: Roseville in relief.

Plate 114
Row 1:
 Frog, #41 . . . . $95.00 – 120.00
 Cornucopia, 6", #143 . . . . $100.00 – 125.00
 Bowl, 4", #387 . . . . $100.00 – 125.00
 Bowl, 3", #653 . . . . $95.00 – 115.00
Row 2:
 Cornucopia, 8", #144 . . . . $125.00 – 150.00
 Basket, 10", #363 . . . . $225.00 – 275.00
 Bowl, 4", #653 . . . . $115.00 – 140.00
 Ewer, 10", #990. . . . . $275.00 – 325.00
Row 3:
 Double Cornucopia, 8", #145 . . . . $125.00 – 150.00
 Tea Set . . . . $400.00 – 500.00
  Teapot, #1-T
  Sugar, #1-S
  Creamer, #1-C
 Vase, 8", #147 . . . . $150.00 – 175.00
Row 4:
 Basket, 12", #364 . . . . $275.00 – 325.00
 Ewer, 15", #993. . . . . $450.00 – 500.00
 Ewer, 6", #981 . . . . $125.00 – 150.00
 Pitcher, #1324 . . . . $225.00 – 250.00

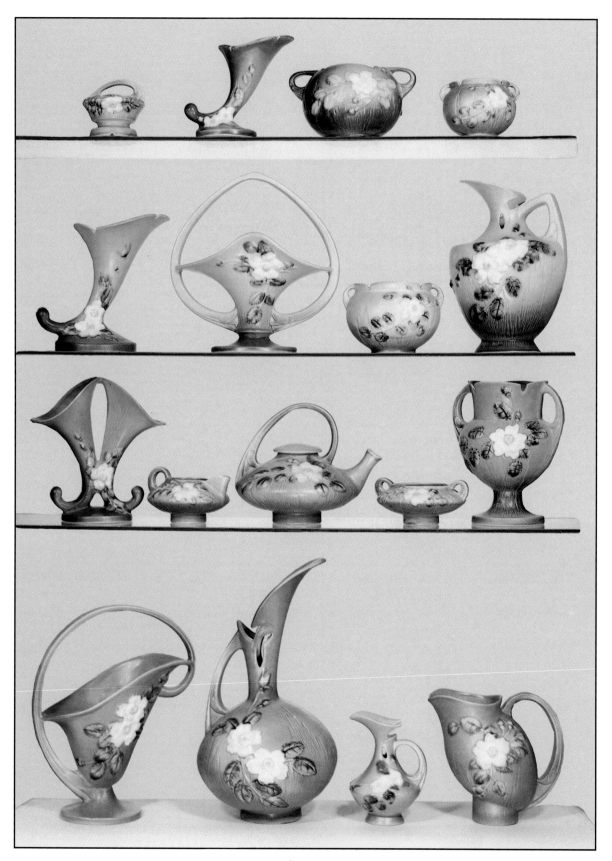

Plate 114

Water Lily
Mark: Roseville in relief.

Plate 115
Row 1:

Jardiniere, 3", #663	Rose with green	$125.00 – 150.00	Blue	$100.00 – 125.00	
	Brown	$85.00 – 100.00			
Ewer, 6", #10	Rose with green	$200.00 – 225.00	Blue	$175.00 – 200.00	
	Brown	$150.00 – 175.00			
Vase, 6", #73	Rose with green	$175.00 – 200.00	Blue	$150.00 – 175.00	
	Brown,	$125.00 – 150.00			
Cornucopia, 6", #177	Rose with green	$175.00 – 200.00	Blue	$150.00 – 175.00	
	Brown	$125.00 – 150.00			

Row 2:

Ewer, 10", #11	Rose with green	$350.00 – 400.00	Blue	$325.00 – 350.00	
	Brown	$300.00 – 325.00			
Cookie Jar, 10", #1	Rose with green	$700.00 – 800.00	Blue	$600.00 – 700.00	
	Brown	$550.00 – 650.00			
Basket, 10", #381	Rose with green	$375.00 – 400.00	Blue	$350.00 – 375.00	
	Brown	$325.00 – 350.00			
Vase, 10", #80	Rose with green	$350.00 – 400.00	Blue	$325.00 – 350.00	
	Brown	$300.00 – 325.00			

Row 3:

Vase, 7", #75	Rose with green	$125.00 – 150.00	Blue	$110.00 – 130.00	
	Brown	$95.00 – 110.00			
Cornucopia, 8", #178	Rose with green	$195.00 – 225.00	Blue	$175.00 – 195.00	
	Brown	$150.00 – 175.00			
Vase, 6", #72	Rose with green	$100.00 – 125.00	Blue	$85.00 – 100.00	
	Brown	$75.00 – 95.00			
Basket, 8", #380	Rose with green	$200.00 – 250.00	Blue	$175.00 – 200.00	
	Brown	$150.00 – 175.00			

Row 4:

Vase, 12", #81	Rose with green	$425.00 – 475.00	Blue	$375.00 – 425.00	
	Brown	$350.00 – 400.00			
Basket, 12", #382	Rose with green	$525.00 – 575.00	Blue	$475.00 – 525.00	
	Brown	$450.00 – 500.00			
Ewer, 15", #12	Rose with green	$900.00 – 1,000.00	Blue	$800.00 – 900.00	
	Brown	$700.00 – 800.00			

Plate 115

Zephyr Lily
Mark: Roseville in relief.

Plate 116
Row 1:
Jardiniere, 4", #671	Blue	$150.00 – 175.00	Brown	$125.00 – 150.00
	Green	$100.00 – 125.00		
Console Boat, 10", #475	Blue	$250.00 – 275.00	Brown	$225.00 – 250.00
	Green	$200.00 – 225.00		
Center Bowl, 8", #474	Blue	$150.00 – 175.00	Brown	$125.00 – 150.00
	Green	$100.00 – 125.00		

Row 2:
Basket, 7", #393	Blue	$175.00 – 200.00	Brown	$150.00 – 175.00
	Green	$125.00 – 150.00		
Cookie Jar, 10", #5	Blue	$750.00 – 850.00	Brown	$600.00 – 675.00
	Green	$500.00 – 550.00		
Ashtray, #29	Blue	$125.00 – 150.00	Brown	$110.00 – 125.00
	Green	$95.00 – 110.00		
Vase, 10", #138	Blue	$250.00 – 275.00	Brown	$225.00 – 250.00
	Green	$200.00 – 225.00		

Row 3:
Basket, 8", #394	Blue	$275.00 – 300.00	Brown	$250.00 – 275.00
	Green	$225.00 – 250.00		
Tea Set (Teapot, Sugar, and Creamer), #7	Blue	$550.00 – 600.00	Brown	$450.00 – 525.00
	Green	$400.00 – 450.00		
Cornucopia, 6", #203	Blue	$150.00 – 175.00	Brown	$125.00 – 150.00
	Green	$100.00 – 125.00		

Row 4:
Basket, 10", #395	Blue	$375.00 – 400.00	Brown	$325.00 – 350.00
	Green	$300.00 – 325.00		
Vase, 7", #131	Blue	$175.00 – 200.00	Brown	$150.00 – 175.00
	Green	$125.00 – 150.00		
Ewer, 15", #24	Blue	$750.00 – 850.00	Brown	$600.00 – 675.00
	Green	$500.00 – 550.00		
Ewer, 10", #23	Blue	$375.00 – 400.00	Brown	$350.00 – 375.00
	Green	$325.00 – 350.00		
Vase, 10", #137	Blue	$325.00 – 350.00	Brown	$300.00 – 325.00
	Green	$275.00 – 300.00		

Plate 116

Peony
Mark: Roseville in relief.

Plate 117
Row 1:
   Bowl, 3", #661 . . . . $95.00 – 125.00
   Vase, 6", #168 . . . . $110.00 – 135.00
   Bowl, 4", #427 . . . . $100.00 – 125.00
Row 2:
   Double Cornucopia, #172 . . . . $125.00 – 150.00
   Basket, 10", #378 . . . . $175.00 – 225.00
   Basket, 7", #376 . . . . $125.00 – 150.00
Row 3:
   Ewer, 6", #7 . . . . $100.00 – 125.00
   Tea Set (Teapot, Sugar, and Creamer), #3 . . . . $400.00 – 450.00
   Bowl, 4", #661 . . . . $100.00 – 125.00
Row 4:
   Vase, 4", #57 . . . . $75.00 – 85.00
   Ewer, 10", #8 . . . . $200.00 – 225.00
   Ewer, 10", #8 . . . . $200.00 – 225.00
   Wall Pocket, 8", #1293 . . . . $250.00 – 300.00

Plate 117

Magnolia
Mark: Roseville in relief.

Plate 118
Row 1:
Planter, 8" wide, #389 . . . . $110.00 – 135.00
Double Bud Vase, 4½", #186 . . . . $100.00 – 125.00
Vase, 4", #86 . . . . $65.00 – 75.00
Bowl, 3", #665 . . . . $65.00 – 75.00
Row 2:
Ewer, 6", #13 . . . . $110.00 – 135.00
Mug, 3", #3 . . . . $125.00 – 150.00
Cider Pitcher, 7", #1327 . . . . $300.00 – 350.00
Mug, 3", #3 . . . . $125.00 – 150.00
Basket, 8", #384 . . . . $150.00 – 200.00
Row 3:
Basket, 7", #383 . . . . $125.00 – 150.00
Tea Set (Pot, Sugar, and Creamer), #4 . . . . $400.00 – 450.00
Row 4:
Basket, 10", #385 . . . . $200.00 – 250.00
Ewer, 15", #15 . . . . $350.00 – 400.00
Cookie Jar, 10", #2 . . . . $450.00 – 550.00

Plate 118

Columbine
Mark: Roseville in relief.

Plate 119
Row 1:

Ewer, 7", #18	. . . . Pink	. . . . $275.00 – 300.00	Blue or Tan	. . . . $225.00 – 250.00
Bowl, 6", #401	. . . . . . Pink	. . . . $150.00 – 175.00	Blue or Tan	. . . . $125.00 – 150.00
Basket, 7", #365	. . . . . Pink	. . . . $275.00 – 300.00	Blue or Tan	. . . . $225.00 – 250.00
Ewer, 7", #18	. . . . Pink	. . . . $275.00 – 300.00	Blue or Tan	. . . . $225.00 – 250.00

Row 2:

Basket, 10", #367	. . . . Pink	. . . . $350.00 – 400.00	Blue or Tan	. . . . $300.00 – 350.00
Bowl, 3", #655	. . . . . . Pink	. . . . $150.00 – 175.00	Blue or Tan	. . . . $100.00 – 125.00
Basket, 12", #368	. . . . Pink	. . . . $450.00 – 500.00	Blue or Tan	. . . . $400.00 – 450.00
Vase, 8", #20	. . . . Pink	. . . . $250.00 – 300.00	Blue or Tan	. . . . $200.00 – 225.00

Plate 119

Foxglove
Marks: Roseville in relief or (rarely) impressed.

Plate 120
Row 1:

Vase, 4", #42	Green w/pink . .	$95.00 – 110.00	Blue . . . $80.00 – 90.00	Pink . . . $70.00 – 80.00
Vase, 3", #659	Green w/pink . . .	$85.00 – 95.00	Blue . . . $75.00 – 85.00	Pink . . . $65.00 – 75.00
Basket, 8", #373 . . .	Green w/pink	$300.00 – 350.00	Blue $250.00 – 275.00	Pink $225.00 – 250.00
Conch Shell,				
6", #426	Green w/pink	$225.00 – 250.00	Blue $200.00 – 225.00	Pink $175.00 – 200.00
Double Bud Vase,				
4½", #160	Green w/pink	$200.00 – 225.00	Blue $175.00 – 200.00	Pink $150.00 – 175.00

Row 2:

Ewer, 6½", #4	Green w/pink	$275.00 – 300.00	Blue $250.00 – 275.00	Pink $225.00 – 250.00
Cornucopia,				
8", #164	Green w/pink	$175.00 – 200.00	Blue $150.00 – 175.00	Pink $140.00 – 160.00
Candle Holders, 4½",				
pair, #1150	Green w/pink	$225.00 – 250.00	Blue $200.00 – 225.00	Pink $175.00 – 200.00
Ewer, 15", #6	Green w/pink	$850.00 – 950.00	Blue $750.00 – 850.00	Pink $700.00 – 800.00
Ewer, 10", #5	Green w/pink	$450.00 – 500.00	Blue $400.00 – 450.00	Pink $375.00 – 400.00

Plate 120

Freesia
Mark: Roseville in relief.

Plate 121
Row 1:
    Ewer, 6", #19 . . . . Green . . . . $275.00 – 325.00   Blue . . . . $250.00 – 275.00
                       Tangerine . . . . . $225.00 – 250.00
    Flowerpot*, 5", #670 . Green . . . . $150.00 – 175.00   Blue . . . . $125.00 – 150.00
                       Tangerine . . . . . $110.00 – 135.00
    Bookends, pair, #15 . . Green . . . . $375.00 – 425.00   Blue . . . . $375.00 – 400.00
                       Tangerine . . . . . $350.00 – 375.00
Row 2:
    Basket, 8", #391 . . . . . Green . . . . $300.00 – 350.00   Blue . . . . $275.00 – 300.00
                       Tangerine . . . . . $250.00 – 275.00
    Pitcher , 10", #20 . . . . Green . . . . $375.00 – 400.00   Blue . . . . $350.00 – 375.00
                       Tangerine . . . . . $325.00 – 350.00
    Basket, 10", #392 . . . . Green . . . . $425.00 – 475.00   Blue . . . . $400.00 – 425.00
                       Tangerine . . . . . $375.00 – 400.00
    Cornucopia, 8", #198 . Green . . . . $175.00 – 200.00   Blue . . . . $150.00 – 175.00
                       Tangerine . . . . . $125.00 – 150.00
Row 3:
    Vase, 8", #122 . . . . Green . . . . $250.00 – 275.00   Blue . . . . $225.00 – 250.00
                       Tangerine . . . . . $200.00 – 225.00
    Tea Set (Pot, Sugar,
        and Creamer), #6 . Green . . . . $500.00 – 550.00   Blue . . . . $450.00 – 500.00
                       Tangerine . . . . . $400.00 – 450.00
    Vase, 7", #120 . . . . Green . . . . $200.00 – 225.00   Blue . . . . $175.00 – 200.00
                       Tangerine . . . . . $160.00 – 170.00
Row 4:
    Cookie Jar, 10", #4 . . . Green . . . . $550.00 – 650.00   Blue . . . . $500.00 – 600.00
                       Tangerine . . . . . $450.00 – 550.00
    Ewer, 15", #21 . . . . . . Green . . . . $850.00 – 950.00   Blue . . . . $750.00 – 850.00
                       Tangerine . . . . . $650.00 – 750.00
    Vase, 8", #196 . . . . Green . . . . $275.00 – 300.00   Blue . . . . $250.00 – 275.00
                       Tangerine . . . . . $225.00 – 250.00
    Candle Holders, 4½",
        pair, #1161 . . . . . . Green . . . . $200.00 – 225.00   Blue . . . . $175.00 – 200.00
                       Tangerine . . . . . $160.00 – 180.00
    Bud Vase, 7", #195 . . . Green . . . . $175.00 – 200.00   Blue . . . . $150.00 – 175.00
                       Tangerine . . . . . $135.00 – 160.00

* Add $75.00 for saucer.

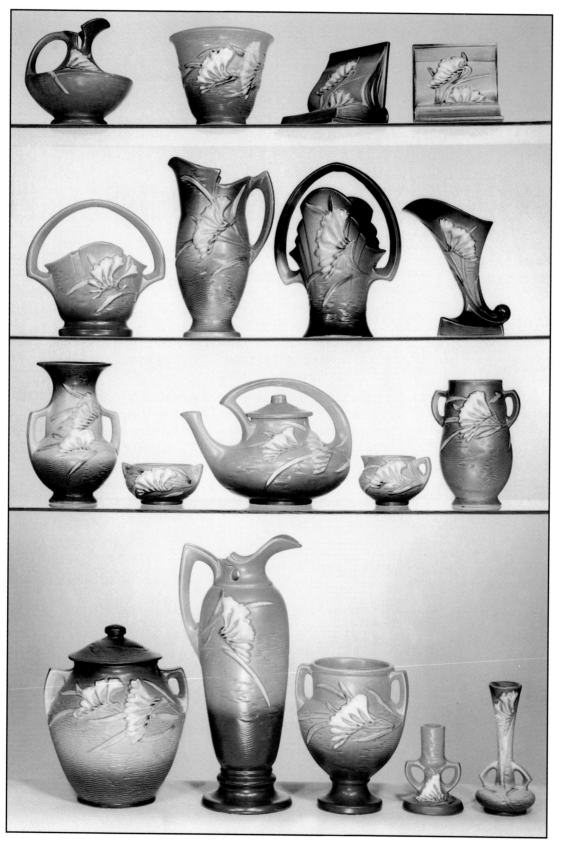

Plate 121

Clematis
Mark: Roseville in relief.

Plate 122
Row 1:
Bowl, 4", #445 . . . . Blue. . . . $75.00 – 100.00   Green or Brown . . . . $60.00 – 75.00
Double Bud Vase, 5", #194 . Blue. . . $125.00 – 150.00   Green or Brown,. . $100.00 – 110.00
Cornucopia, 6", #190 . . . . . . Blue. . . $100.00 – 125.00   Green or Brown . . . $90.00 – 110.00
Candle Holders,
    4½", pair, #1159 . . . . . . Blue. . . $150.00 – 175.00   Green or Brown . . $110.00 – 130.00
Row 2:
Basket, 8", #388 . . . . Blue. . . $250.00 – 275.00   Green or Brown . . $200.00 – 225.00
Bud Vase, 7", #187 . . . . Blue. . . $150.00 – 175.00   Green or Brown . . $125.00 – 150.00
Ewer, 10" , #17 . . . . Blue. . . $250.00 – 275.00   Green or Brown . . $200.00 – 225.00
Basket, 7", #387 . . . . Blue. . . $225.00 – 250.00   Green or Brown . . $175.00 – 200.00
Ewer, 6", #16 . . . . Blue. . . $175.00 – 200.00   Green or Brown . . $150.00 – 160.00
Row 3:
Vase, 8", #108 . . . . Blue. . . $150.00 – 175.00   Green or Brown . . $120.00 – 140.00
Tea Set, (Pot, Sugar,
    and Creamer), #5 . . . . . Blue. . . $450.00 – 500.00   Green or Brown . . $375.00 – 425.00
Vase, 6", #188 . . . . Blue. . . $125.00 – 150.00   Green or Brown . . $100.00 – 110.00
Row 4:
Cookie Jar, 10", #3 . . . . Blue. . . $500.00 – 550.00   Green or Brown . . $400.00 – 450.00
Wall Pocket, 8", #1295 . . . . Blue. . . $225.00 – 250.00   Green or Brown . . $200.00 – 225.00
Ewer, 15", #18 . . . . Blue. . . $450.00 – 500.00   Green or Brown . . $400.00 – 450.00
Basket, 10", #389 . . . . Blue. . . $300.00 – 325.00   Green or Brown . . $250.00 – 275.00

Plate 122

Apple Blossom
Mark: Roseville in relief.

Plate 123
Row 1:

Cornucopia, 6", #321 . . . Blue . . . . $150.00 – 175.00   Pink or Green . $125.00 – 150.00
Hanging Basket, #361 . . Blue . . . . $350.00 – 400.00   Pink or Green . $300.00 – 350.00
Vase, 6", #381 . . . . Blue . . . . . . $150.00 – 175.00   Pink or Green . $125.00 – 150.00

Row 2:

Tea Set (Pot, Sugar,
and Creamer), #371 . Blue . . . . $650.00 – 750.00   Pink or Green . $550.00 – 650.00
Basket, 8", #309 . . . . Blue . . . . . . $325.00 – 375.00   Pink or Green . $275.00 – 325.00

Row 3:

Ewer, 8", #316 . . . . Blue . . . . $275.00 – 325.00   Pink or Green . $225.00 – 275.00
Vase, 7", #382 . . . . Blue . . . . . . $175.00 – 200.00   Pink or Green . $150.00 – 175.00
Basket, 10", #310 . . . . . Blue . . . . . . $425.00 – 475.00   Pink or Green . $375.00 – 425.00
Bud Vase, 7", #379 . . . . Blue . . . . . . $175.00 – 200.00   Pink or Green . $150.00 – 175.00

Row 4:

Vase, 9", #387 . . . . Blue . . . . . . $325.00 – 375.00   Pink or Green . $275.00 – 325.00
Ewer, 15", #318. . . . . . . Blue . . . . . . $900.00 – 1,000.00   Pink or Green . $800.00 – 900.00
Basket, 12", #311 . . . . . Blue . . . . . . $525.00 – 575.00   Pink or Green . $450.00 – 500.00

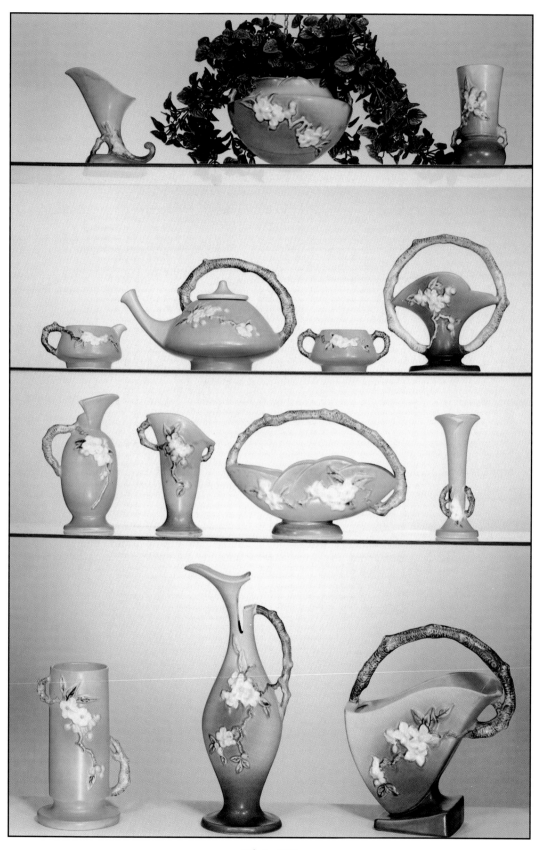

Plate 123

Bushberry
Mark: Roseville in relief.

Plate 124
Row 1:

Bowl, 4", #411 . . . . . . Blue. . . . . $150.00 – 175.00   Green . . . . $125.00 – 150.00
Orange . . . . $100.00 – 125.00

Basket, 6½", #369 . . . Blue. . . . . $300.00 – 325.00   Green . . . . $250.00 – 275.00
Orange . . . . $200.00 – 225.00

Cornucopia, 6", #153 . Blue. . . . . $150.00 – 175.00   Green . . . . $125.00 – 150.00
Orange . . . . $100.00 – 125.00

Vase, 6", #29. . . . . . . Blue. . . . . $150.00 – 175.00   Green . . . . $125.00 – 150.00
Orange . . . . $100.00 – 125.00

Jardiniere, 3", #657 . . Blue. . . . . $125.00 – 150.00   Green . . . . $100.00 – 125.00
Orange . . . . $80.00 – 90.00

Row 2:

Ewer, 6", #1 . . . . Blue. . . . . $175.00 – 200.00   Green . . . . $150.00 – 175.00
Orange . . . . $125.00 – 150.00

Cornucopia, #3 . . . . . Blue. . . . . $200.00 – 225.00   Green . . . . $175.00 – 200.00
Orange . . . . $150.00 – 175.00

Wall Pocket, 8", #1291 Blue. . . . . $550.00 – 600.00   Green . . . . $450.00 – 500.00
Orange . . . . $400.00 – 450.00

Basket, 8", #370 . . . . Blue. . . . . $300.00 – 350.00   Green . . . . $250.00 – 300.00
Orange . . . . $200.00 – 250.00

Row 3:

Tea Set (Pot, Sugar,
and Creamer), #2. Blue. . . . . $600.00 – 700.00   Green . . . . $500.00 – 600.00
Orange . . . . $450.00 – 500.00

Row 4:

Ewer, 10", #2 . . . . Blue. . . . . $400.00 – 450.00   Green . . . . $350.00 – 400.00
Orange . . . . $300.00 – 350.00

Basket, 12", #372 . . . . Blue. . . . . $450.00 – 500.00   Green . . . . $400.00 – 450.00
Orange . . . . $350.00 – 400.00

Cornucopia, 8", #154 . Blue. . . . . $175.00 – 200.00   Green . . . . $150.00 – 175.00
Orange . . . . $125.00 – 150.00

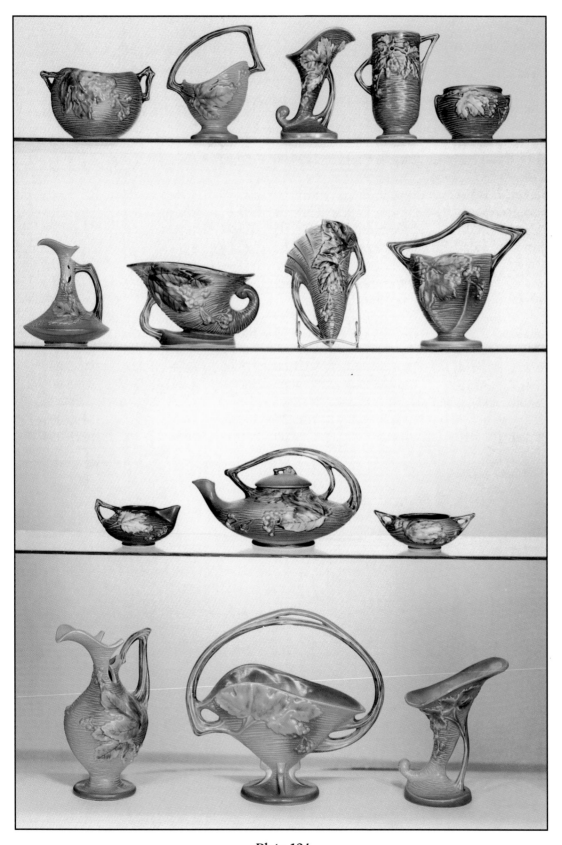

Plate 124

Snowberry
Mark: Roseville in relief.

Plate 125
Row 1:
    Ashtray, #1AT. . . . . . . Blue or Pink. . . $150.00 – 175.00   Green . . . . $125.00 – 150.00
    Center Bowl,
        10" wide, #1BL1. . Blue or Pink. . . $150.00 – 175.00   Green . . . . $125.00 – 150.00
    Ewer, 6", #1TK. . . . . . Blue or Pink. . . $125.00 – 150.00   Green . . . . $100.00 – 125.00
Row 2:
    Basket, 7", #1BK . . . . Blue or Pink. . . $150.00 – 175.00   Green . . . . $125.00 – 150.00
    Cornucopia, 6", #1CC. Blue or Pink. . . $100.00 – 125.00   Green . . . . $90.00 – 110.00
    Basket, 8", #1BK . . . . Blue or Pink. . . $250.00 – 275.00   Green . . . . $225.00 – 250.00
    Rose Bowl, 5", #1RB . Blue or Pink. . . $150.00 – 175.00   Green . . . . $125.00 – 150.00
Row 3:
    Ewer, 6", #1TK. . . . . . Blue or Pink. . . $150.00 – 175.00   Green, ... $125.00 – 150.00
    Tea Set (Pot, Sugar, and Creamer), Shape Nos. 1TP, 1S, 1C
                Blue or Pink. . . $450.00 – 500.00   Green . . . . $400.00 – 450.00
    Bud Vase, 7", #1BV. . . Blue or Pink. . . $100.00 – 120.00   Green . . . . $85.00 – 95.00
Row 4:
    Basket, 8", #1BK . . . . Blue or Pink. . . $250.00 – 275.00   Green . . . . $225.00 – 250.00
    Ewer, 10", #1TK. . . . . Blue or Pink. . . $300.00 – 350.00   Green . . . . $250.00 – 275.00
    Candle Holders, pair, #1CS1
                Blue or Pink. . . $125.00 – 150.00   Green . . . . $100.00 – 125.00
    Basket, 10", #1BK . . . Blue or Pink. . . $300.00 – 350.00   Green . . . . $275.00 – 300.00

Plate 125

Mayfair
Mark: Roseville in relief.

Plate 126

Bowl, 4", #1110 . . . . $50.00 – 75.00
Pitcher, 8", #1105. . . . . $150.00 – 175.00
Tankard, 12", #1107 . . . . $175.00 – 200.00
Planter, 8", #1113. . . . . $60.00 – 75.00

Mock Orange
Mark: Roseville, U. S. A. Mock Orange in relief.

Plate 127
Row 1:

Jardiniere, 4", #900 . . . . $75.00 – 100.00
Basket, 6", #908 . . . . $125.00 – 150.00
Ewer, 6", #916 . . . . $125.00 – 150.00
Row 2:
Planter, 7", #981. . . . . $150.00 – 175.00
Row 3:
Basket, 8", #909, each. . . . . $250.00 – 300.00

Plate 126

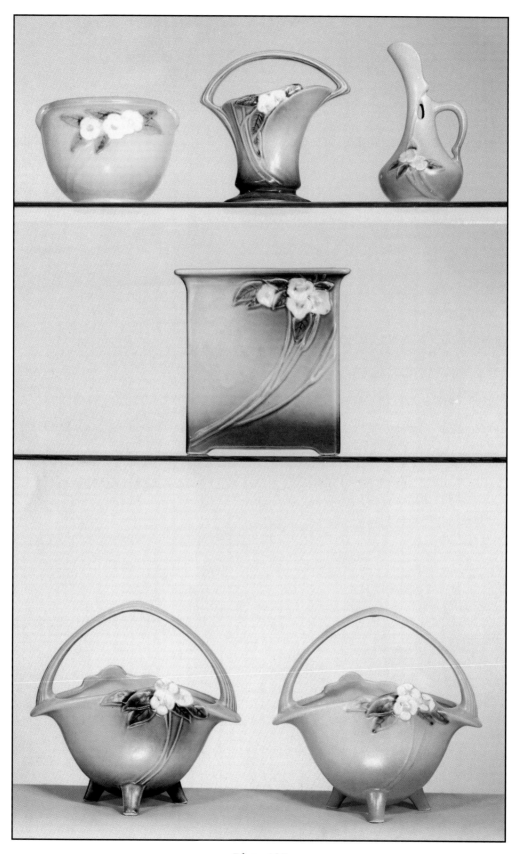

Plate 127

Burmese
Marks: R or Roseville in relief.

Plate 128

Candle Holder/Bookends, pair,
    White, #82-B . . . . $225.00 – 250.00
    Black, #70-B. . . . . $250.00 – 275.00
Candlestick (in center), #75-B . . . . $50.00 – 60.00

Royal Capri
Mark: Roseville in relief.

Plate 129

Bowl, 7", #GR-526. (Gold MUST be excellent) . . . . $300.00 – 350.00

Ming Tree
Mark: Roseville in relief.

Plate 130
Row 1:
    Candle Holders, extreme left and right, pair, #551 . . . . $100.00 – 125.00
    Basket, 8", #508 . . . . $125.00 – 150.00
Row 2:
    Center Bowl, 10" across, #528 . . . . $125.00 – 150.00
Row 3:
    Vase, 8", #582 . . . . $100.00 – 125.00
    Ewer, 10", #516. . . . . $150.00 – 175.00
    Vase, 6", #581 . . . . $75.00 – 85.00

Plate 128

Plate 129

Plate 134

Plate 135

Silhouette
Mark: Roseville in relief.

Plate 136
Row 1:
    Candle Holders, extreme left and right, 3", pair, #751 . . . . $100.00 – 125.00
    Planter, 14" long, #731 . . . .$125.00 – 150.00
Row 2:
    Planter Vase, 5", #756 . . . . $85.00 – 95.00
    Ewer, 6", #716 . . . .$100.00 – 125.00
    Ewer, 10", #717 . . . .$175.00 – 200.00
    Basket, 6", #708 . . . .$150.00 – 175.00
    Vase, 7", #782 . . . . $85.00 – 95.00
Row 3:
    Cornucopia, 8", #721 . . . . $85.00 – 95.00
    Fan Vase, 7", #783 . . . .$400.00 – 450.00
    Ashtray, #799 . . . . $75.00 – 85.00
    Basket, 8", #709 . . . .$175.00 – 200.00
Row 4:
    Basket, 10", #710 . . . .$250.00 – 300.00
    Cigarette Box, #740 . . . .$150.00 – 175.00
    Vase, 8", #763 . . . .$500.00 – 650.00
    Vase, 9", #785 . . . .$150.00 – 175.00
    Wall Pocket, 8", #766 . . . .$225.00 – 275.00

Plate 136

Wincraft
Mark: Roseville in relief.

Plate 137
Row 1:
    Planter Set, 6", #1051 and #1050 . . . . $175.00 – 225.00
    Tea Set (Pot, Sugar, and Creamer), #271 . . . . $225.00 – 250.00
Row 2:
    Basket, 12", #209 . . . . $175.00 – 200.00
    Candle Holders, pair, #2CS. . . . . $75.00 – 85.00
    ARTWOOD Circle Vase, 8", #1053. . . . . $150.00 – 175.00
    Ewer, 8", #216 . . . . $125.00 – 150.00
Row 3:
    Planter, 10", #231 . . . . $125.00 – 150.00
    Cornucopia, 8", #222 . . . . $125.00 – 150.00
    Ewer, 6", #217 . . . . $95.00 – 105.00
    Basket, 8", #208 . . . . $150.00 – 175.00
Row 4:
    Vase, 8", #282 . . . . $150.00 – 175.00
    Vase, 10", #284 . . . . $225.00 – 250.00
    Vase, 10", #290. . . . . $900.00 – 1,000.00
    Vase, 10", #285 . . . . $200.00 – 250.00
    Vase, 6", #272 . . . . $95.00 – 105.00

Plate 137

Raymor
Mark: Raymor by Roseville, U. S. A. in relief.

Plate 138

Bean Pot, #195...$50.00 – 60.00
Swinging Coffeepot, #176...$450.00 – 500.00
Bean Pot, #194...$60.00 – 70.00

Plate 139
Row 1:
Hot Plate, #84-198 and Casserole, #198...........................$75.00 – 85.00
Hot Plate, #159 ....$35.00 – 40.00
Cup and Saucer, #151...$25.00 – 30.00
Row 2:
Tea Set (Sugar, #157; Creamer, #158)............................$250.00 – 300.00
Row 3:
Salad Plate, #154 ....$15.00 – 20.00
Dinner Plate, #152..$20.00 – 30.00
Luncheon Plate, #153 ....$15.00 – 20.00

Plate 138

Plate 139

Jardinieres and Pedestals, Umbrella Stands

Plate 140

      33" BLACKBERRY set (12" jardiniere) . . . . $5,000.00 – 6,000.00

  * 29" BLACKBERRY set (10" jardiniere) . . . . $3,500.00 – 4,500.00

      29" DONATELLO set (10" jardiniere) . . . . $1,000.00 – 1,100.00

      30" PINE CONE set (10" jardiniere).

        Blue . . . $4,500.00 – 5,500.00   Brown . . . $3,000.00 – 3,500.00   Green . . . $2,500.00 – 3,000.00

  * 33½" PINE CONE set (12" jardiniere).

        Blue . . . $6,000.00 – 7,000.00   Brown . . . $4,500.00 – 5,500.00   Green . . . $3,500.00 – 4,500.00

  * 24" PINE CONE set (8" jardiniere).

        Blue . . . $3,000.00 – 4,000.00   Brown . . . $2,000.00 – 2,500.00   Green . . . $1,750.00 – 2,250.00

      32" MAGNOLIA set (10" jardiniere).

        With handles:

        Blue . . . $2,000.00 – 2,500.00   Green . . . $1,750.00 – 2,000.00   Brown . . . $1,500.00 – 1,750.00

        * Without handles:

        Blue . . . $1,750.00 – 2,000.00   Green . . . $1,500.00 – 1,750.00   Brown . . . $1,250.00 – 1,500.00

  * 24" MAGNOLIA set (8" jardiniere).

        With handles:

        Blue . . . $1,250.00 – 1,500.00   Green . . . $1,100.00 – 1,250.00   Brown . . . . $900.00 – 1,150.00

        Without handles:

        Blue . . . $1,100.00 – 1,250.00   Green . . . . . $950.00 – 1,100.00   Brown . . . . . . $800.00 – 950.00

Plate 141

      MOSTIQUE Umbrella Stand . . . . $800.00 – 900.00

      28½", MOSTIQUE set, (this style only) . . . . $1,250.00 – 1,500.00

      31", FUCHSIA set, 31" set (10" jardiniere).

        Blue . . . $4,500.00 – 5,500.00   Green . . . $3,000.00 – 3,500.00   Brown/Tan$2,500.00 – 3,000.00

  * 24", FUCHSIA set (8" jardiniere).

        Blue . . . $2,500.00 – 3,000.00   Green . . . $1,750.00 – 2,000.00   Brown/Tan$1,500.00 – 1,750.00

      24", FREESIA set (8" jardiniere).

        Blue . . . $1,250.00 – 1,500.00   Green . . . $1,000.00 – 1,200.00   Tangerine . . $900.00 – 1,100.00

  * Not shown.

Plate 140

Plate 141

Miscellaneous

Plate 142
　　Factory Lamp, foil sticker. . . . .$850.00 – 950.00

Plate 143
　　MODERNE Trial Glaze Vase, 8", #796, Roseville impressed . . . .$600.00 – 700.00

Plate 144
　　CRYSTAL GREEN Vase, 8", #942, Roseville impressed . . . .$150.00 – 200.00

Plate 145
　　CAPRI Basket, 10", #C-1012 . . . .$100.00 – 150.00

Plate 146
　　VISTA Basket, 8", foil sticker . . . .$800.00 – 900.00

Plate 142

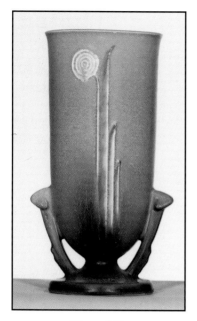

Plate 143

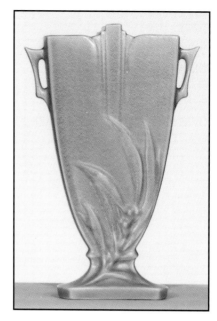

Plate 144

Plate 145

Plate 146

Umbrella Stands and Sand Jars

Plate 147

IMPERIAL I, Umbrella Stand. . . . . $900.00 – 1,000.00
FLORENTINE, Umbrella Stand. . . . . $1,000.00 – 1,250.00
PINE CONE, Umbrella Stand
    Green . . . $1,750.00 – 2,250.00   Brown . . . . $2,500.00 – 3,000.00   Blue $3,000.00 – 3,500.00
FLORENTINE II, Sand Jar, Roseville in relief . . . . $900.00 – 1,000.00

Plate 147

This section contains reproductions of the color plates in the old Roseville catalogs. Some are of seldom seen lines; others are of those lines that are so diversified and dissimilar as to make proper identification difficult.

Many catalog pages were colored with what appeared to be a thin tint over a black and white photo; in many cases, the colors were evidently not entirely accurate. On some pages, only the bisque shapes were shown, unglazed and without any attempt at color. Two of these were Luffa and Russco. Victorian Art Pottery was shown in only white, blank shape outlines. We have since learned that this was a line designed to be tailored to customer preference with a choice of decoration: scarabs, grapes and leaves, and sailing ships — thus the blank shapes on the catalog page.

Complete lines are not shown, but through comparisons of shapes, handles, glaze texture, etc., these pages may help the collector to identify many of the more unusual pieces.

Autumn, Before 1916

Azurine, Orchid, and Turquoise, 1920 (?)

Banks, Early 1900s

Banks, Early 1900s

Blue Teapots, Before 1916

Carnelian II, 1915

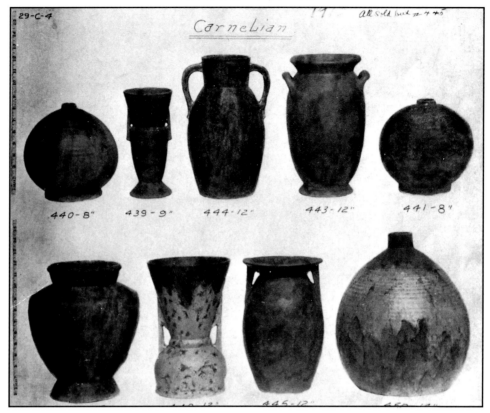

Cameo, 1920

Cameo, 1920

Chloron, 1907

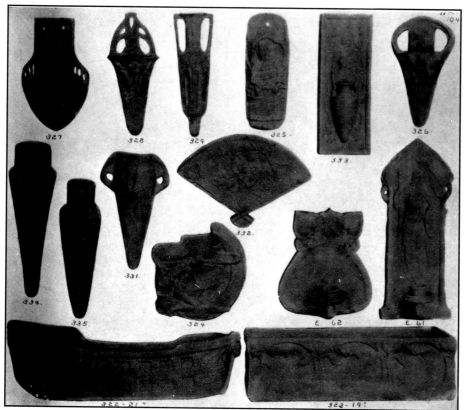

Chloron, 1907

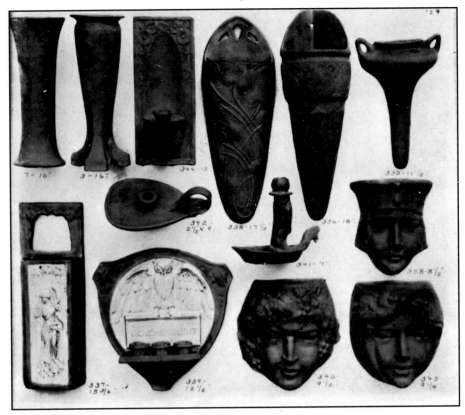

Colonial Toilet Set, 1900s

Cremo, 1916

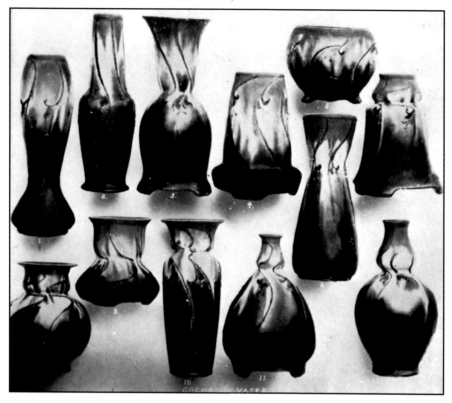

Crystalis (Rozane), 1906

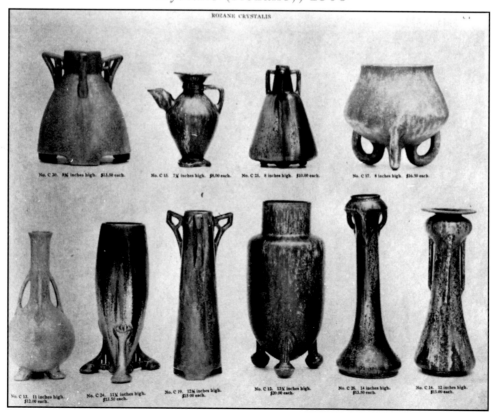

Della Robbia Teapots, 1905

Della Robbia (Rozane), 1905

Egypto (Rozane), 1905

Earlam, 1930

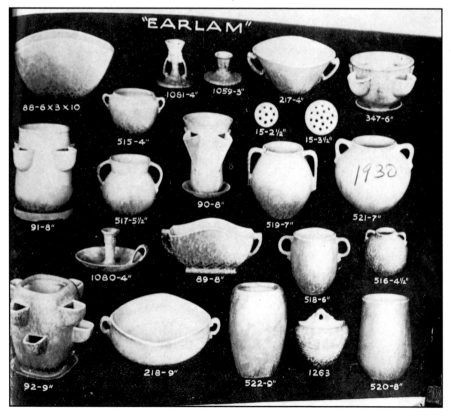

Earlam, 1930

Early Pitchers, Before 1916

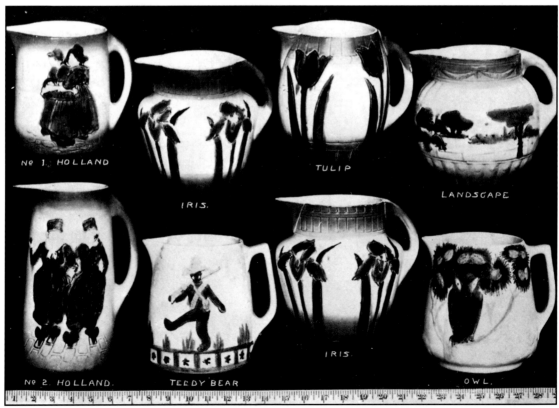

Early Pitchers, Before 1916

Futura, 1928

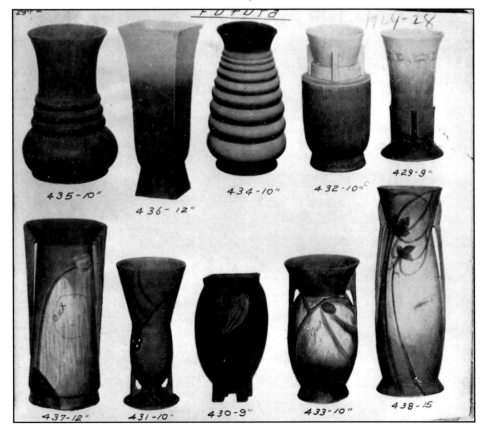

435-10"

436-12"

434-10"

432-10"

429-9"

437-12"

431-10"

430-9"

433-10"

438-15

Futura, 1928

Futura, 1928

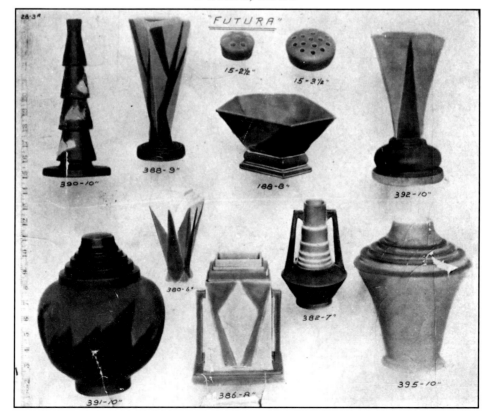

Futura, 1928

Futura, 1928

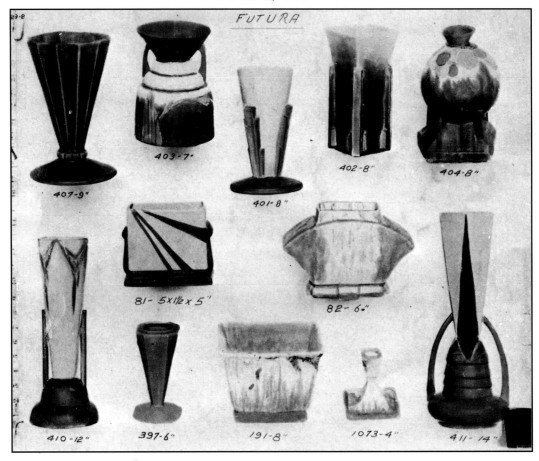

Garden Pottery, 1931

Gold Traced, Before 1916

Holland, Before 1916

Individual Tea Sets, Before 1916

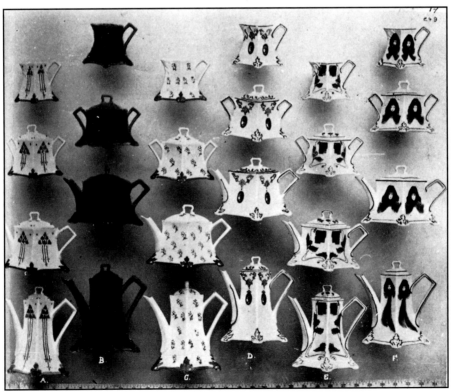

Imperial II, 1924

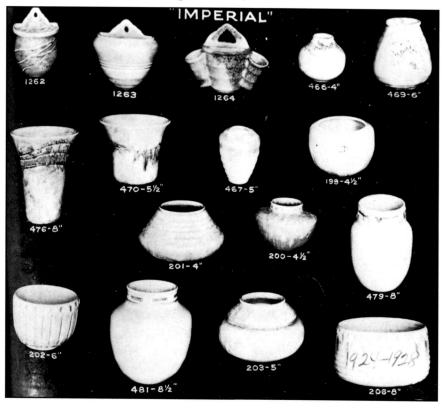

Imperial II, 1924

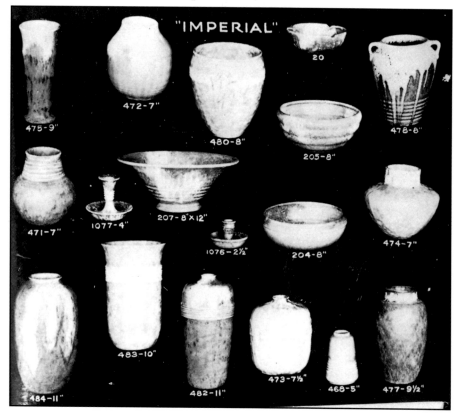

Juvenile, 1916 – 1935

Juvenile, 1916 – 1935

Lombardy, 1924

Lombardy, 1924

Lustre, 1921

Lustre, 1921

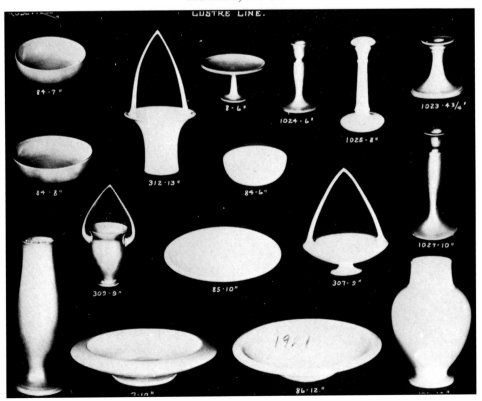

Jardinieres and Pedestals, Early 1900s

Matt Color, 1920s

Moderne, 1930s

Novelty Steins, Before 1916

Opac Enamels, 1900

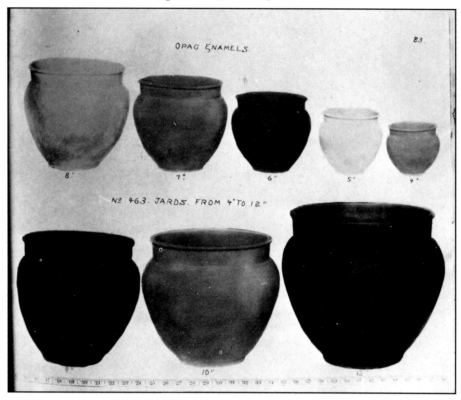

Rozane Pattern, 1940s

Rosecraft, 1920s

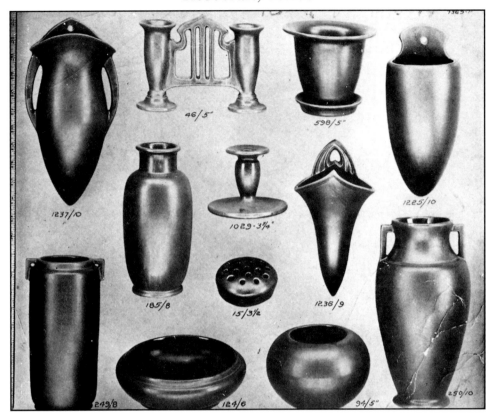

Rosecraft Black, 1916

Savona, 1924 – 1928

Sylvan, 1918

Sylvan, 1918

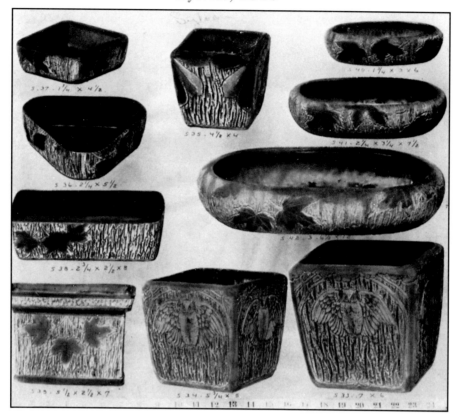

Sylvan, 1918

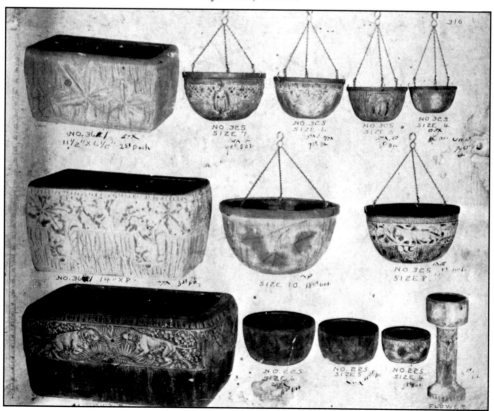

Tourmaline, 1933

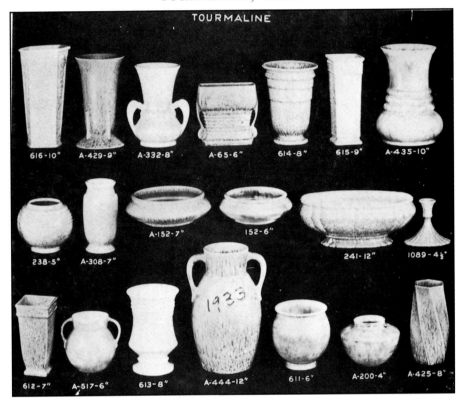

Umbrella Stands, Early 1900s

Victorian Art Pottery, 1924 – 1928

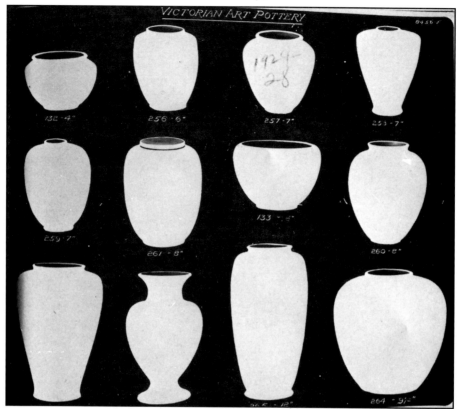

Venetian, Early 1900s

Shown in composite below, pudding crock and bake pans, spongeware is Cornelian, early 1900s.

Volpato, 1918

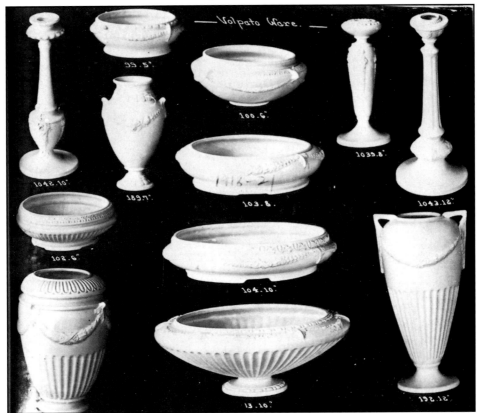

Volpato, 1918

Alexander, Donald E.
Roseville Pottery for Collectors.
Published by the author, 1970.

Bassett, Mark.
Introducing Roseville Pottery.
Schiffer Publishing Ltd., 1999.

Buxton, Virginia
Private correspondence.

Cobb, Lura Milburn.
A Visit to Some Zaneville Potteries.
The Southwestern Book, December, 1905.

Cox, Warrren E.
The Book of Pottery and Porcelain.
Crown Publishers, 1970.

Evans, Paul.
Art Pottery of the United States.
Crown Publishers, 1975.

Hall, Francis and Gladys.
Hall's Pricing Formulas.
Published by the authors.

Henzke, Lucile.
American Art Pottery.
Thomas Nelson, Inc., 1970.

Kovel, Ralph and Terry.
The Kovels' Collector's Guide to American Art Pottery.
Crown Publishers, Inc., 1974.

Muskingum Company bibliography, 1905.

Ohio Historical Society.
Roseville records and daily ledger.

Peck, Herbert.
The Book of Rookwood Pottery.
Bonanza Books, 1968.

Purviance, Louise and Evan, and Norris F. Schneider.
Roseville Art Pottery in Color.
Wallace-Homestead Book Co., 1970.

Schneider, Norris
Zanesville Art Pottery.
Published by the author, 1963.

Art Pottery – True form of art, unique in shape or decoration motivated by free expression of one's artistic abilities.

Bisque – Ceramic wares, not yet decorated, having been subjected to only one firing for the purpose of hardening the clay.

Body – Term referring to the particular type and characteristics of the material forming a vessel.

Ceramics – Term used to cover a variety of fired, clay products.

Crazing – The crackled appearance of certain glazes caused by uneven expansion and contractions between body and glaze.

Creamware – Type of highly refined earthenware body, very light in color.

Decalcomania – A picture or design transferred from prepared paper, a decal.

Decorator – One who applies color to a pre-determined design.

Designer – One who develops and sketches proposed shapes; may also draw up actual working patterns.

Embossing – Raised design formed on the surface of an item within the mold.

Finisher – One who sponges and smooths out defects in the unfired ware.

Glaze – The glassy finish applied to the decorated surface of pottery as a liquid and fired in the kiln until it becomes a hard and protective covering.

Jigger – Type of molding machine consisting of a paddle or stick which is lowered into the mold, pressing the clay into the sides of mold while it is spinning on the wheel.

Lustre – A glaze with the patina of metals, produced through the use of metallic oxides.

Molds – Sectional forms which are used to shape pottery, either by casting, in which case liquid clay or slip is poured into the mold, allowed to stand until desired thickness adheres to the wall of the mold, the excess then poured out; or by jiggering.

Muffle Kiln – Oven used to permanently affix decoration or color on pottery, operates at a relatively low temperature.

Overglaze – Method of decorating on top of the glaze and refiring at a low temperature, causing the decoration to become permanent.

Porcelain – A high content silica mixture which is soft fired, leaving a porous body that readily absorbs glaze and becomes translucent when refired; china.

Pottery – Earthenware that contains less silica than porcelain, and when fired, becomes so dense it will not absorb the glaze; the body remains opaque.

Pouncing – Method which uses waxed patterns, perforated to allow powdered talc to sift through, to transfer the outlines of the design to the surface of the ware; designs are then completed by the decorator.

Sagger – Boxes in which unfired ware was placed, used to protect the pottery as it was fired in the kiln.

Sang de Beouf – Literal meaning, ox blood; copper glaze resulting in a true red color.

Second – Any item not meeting standard quality control as first grade but without serious imperfections.

Sgraffito – Method of decoration where the pattern is incised into an outer layer of clay, thereby exposing a second layer of color.

Slip – Mixture of clay and water used for casting in the mold; colored and used for painting; or in a heavier consistency, forced through a device to make threads of clay used to decorate the surface of the pottery.

Slip Ware – Pottery decorated by the squeeze-bag technique, wherein slender threads of soft, colored clay are piped on over an existing background color.

Underglaze Decoration – Method of decorating pottery using colored slip before the glazing process.

Numbers indicate pages in the Color Album of Pottery; catalog reprints are noted within brackets. Lines designated NP are not pictured in this book; see Volume II. Each line is fully described and their color assortments listed on pages 23 through 29. Production spans are given there as well.

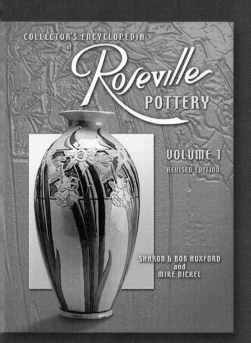
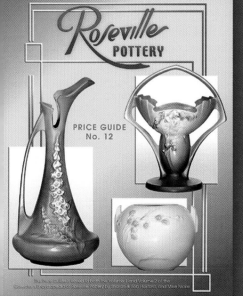

COLLECTOR BOOKS

Informing Today's Collector

For over two decades we have been keeping collectors informed on trends and values in all fields of antiques and collectibles.

DOLLS, FIGURES & TEDDY BEARS

4707	A Decade of **Barbie Dolls** & Collectibles, 1981–1991, Summers	$19.95
4631	**Barbie Doll** Boom, 1986–1995, Augustyniak	$18.95
2079	**Barbie Doll** Fashion, Volume I, Eames	$24.95
4846	**Barbie Doll** Fashion, Volume II, Eames	$24.95
3957	**Barbie** Exclusives, Rana	$18.95
4632	**Barbie** Exclusives, Book II, Rana	$18.95
5672	The **Barbie Doll** Years, 4th Ed., Olds	$19.95
3810	**Chatty Cathy** Dolls, Lewis	$15.95
5352	Collector's Ency. of **Barbie** Doll Exclusives & More, 2nd Ed.,Augustyniak	$24.95
2211	Collector's Encyclopedia of **Madame Alexander** Dolls, Smith	$24.95
4863	Collector's Encyclopedia of **Vogue Dolls**, Izen/Stover	$29.95
5821	**Doll Values**, Antique to Modern, 5th Ed., Moyer	$12.95
5829	**Madame Alexander** Collector's Dolls Price Guide #26, Crowsey	$12.95
5833	**Modern Collectible Dolls**, Volume V, Moyer	$24.95
5689	**Nippon Dolls** & Playthings, Van Patten/Lau	$29.95
5365	**Peanuts Collectibles**, Podley/Bang	$24.95
5253	Story of **Barbie**, 2nd Ed., Westenhouser	$24.95
5277	**Talking Toys** of the 20th Century, Lewis	$15.95
1513	**Teddy Bears & Steiff** Animals, Mandel	$9.95
1817	**Teddy Bears & Steiff** Animals, 2nd Series, Mandel	$19.95
2084	**Teddy Bears, Annalee's & Steiff** Animals, 3rd Series, Mandel	$19.95
5371	**Teddy Bear** Treasury, Yenke	$19.95
1808	Wonder of **Barbie**, Manos	$9.95
1430	World of **Barbie** Dolls, Manos	$9.95
4880	World of **Raggedy Ann** Collectibles, Avery	$24.95

TOYS, MARBLES & CHRISTMAS COLLECTIBLES

2333	Antique & Collectible **Marbles**, 3rd Ed., Grist	$9.95
5353	**Breyer Animal** Collector's Guide, 2nd Ed., Browell	$19.95
4976	**Christmas Ornaments**, Lights & Decorations, Johnson	$24.95
4737	**Christmas Ornaments**, Lights & Decorations, Vol. II, Johnson	$24.95
4739	**Christmas Ornaments**, Lights & Decorations, Vol. III, Johnson	$24.95
4559	Collectible **Action Figures**, 2nd Ed., Manos	$17.95
2338	Collector's Encyclopedia of **Disneyana**, Longest, Stern	$24.95
5038	Collector's Guide to **Diecast Toys** & Scale Models, 2nd Ed., Johnson	$19.95
4651	Collector's Guide to **Tinker Toys**, Strange	$18.95
4566	Collector's Guide to **Tootsietoys**, 2nd Ed., Richter	$19.95
5169	Collector's Guide to **TV Toys** & Memorabilia, 2nd Ed., Davis/Morgan	$24.95
5360	**Fisher-Price Toys**, Cassity	$19.95
4720	The Golden Age of **Automotive Toys**, 1925–1941, Hutchison/Johnson	$24.95
5593	Grist's Big Book of **Marbles**, 2nd Ed.	$24.95
3970	Grist's Machine-Made & Contemporary **Marbles**, 2nd Ed.	$9.95
5267	**Matchbox Toys**, 1947 to 1998, 3rd Ed., Johnson	$19.95
5830	**McDonald's** Collectibles, 2nd Edition, Henriques/DuVall	$24.95
5673	Modern **Candy Containers** & Novelties, Brush/Miller	$19.95
1540	Modern **Toys** 1930–1980, Baker	$19.95
3888	**Motorcycle Toys**, Antique & Contemporary, Gentry/Downs	$18.95
5693	**Schroeder's Collectible Toys**, Antique to Modern Price Guide, 7th Ed.	$17.95

FURNITURE

1457	American **Oak** Furniture, McNerney	$9.95
3716	American **Oak** Furniture, Book II, McNerney	$12.95
1118	Antique **Oak** Furniture, Hill	$7.95
2271	Collector's Encyclopedia of **American** Furniture, Vol. II, Swedberg	$24.95
3720	Collector's Encyclopedia of **American** Furniture, Vol. III, Swedberg	$24.95
5359	Early **American** Furniture, Obbard	$12.95
1755	Furniture of the **Depression Era**, Swedberg	$19.95
3906	**Heywood-Wakefield** Modern Furniture, Rouland	$18.95
1885	**Victorian** Furniture, Our American Heritage, McNerney	$9.95
3829	**Victorian** Furniture, Our American Heritage, Book II, McNerney	$9.95

JEWELRY, HATPINS, WATCHES & PURSES

1712	Antique & Collectible **Thimbles** & Accessories, Mathis	$19.95
1748	Antique **Purses**, Revised Second Ed., Holiner	$19.95
1278	Art Nouveau & Art Deco **Jewelry**, Baker	$9.95
4850	Collectible **Costume Jewelry**, Simonds	$24.95
5675	Collectible **Silver Jewelry**, Rezazadeh	$24.95
3722	Collector's Ency. of **Compacts**, Carryalls & Face Powder Boxes, Mueller	$24.95
4940	**Costume Jewelry**, A Practical Handbook & Value Guide, Rezazadeh	$24.95
1716	Fifty Years of Collectible **Fashion Jewelry**, 1925–1975, Baker	$19.95
1424	**Hatpins** & Hatpin Holders, Baker	$9.95
5695	**Ladies' Vintage Accessories**, Bruton	$24.95
1181	100 Years of Collectible **Jewelry**, 1850–1950, Baker	$9.95
4729	**Sewing Tools** & Trinkets, Thompson	$24.95
5620	Unsigned Beauties of **Costume Jewelry**, Brown	$24.95
4878	Vintage & Contemporary **Purse Accessories**, Gerson	$24.95
5696	Vintage & Vogue Ladies' **Compacts**, 2nd Edition, Gerson	$29.95

INDIANS, GUNS, KNIVES, TOOLS, PRIMITIVES

1868	Antique **Tools**, Our American Heritage, McNerney	$9.95
5616	Big Book of **Pocket Knives**, Stewart	$19.95
4943	Field Guide to Flint **Arrowheads** & Knives of the North American Indian	$9.95
2279	**Indian Artifacts** of the Midwest, Book I, Hothem	$14.95
3885	**Indian Artifacts** of the Midwest, Book II, Hothem	$16.95
4870	**Indian Artifacts** of the Midwest, Book III, Hothem	$18.95
5685	**Indian Artifacts** of the Midwest, Book IV, Hothem	$19.95
5687	**Modern Guns**, Identification & Values, 13th Ed., Quertermous	$14.95
2164	**Primitives**, Our American Heritage, McNerney	$9.95
1759	**Primitives**, Our American Heritage, 2nd Series, McNerney	$14.95
4730	Standard **Knife** Collector's Guide, 3rd Ed., Ritchie & Stewart	$12.95

PAPER COLLECTIBLES & BOOKS

4633	Big Little Books, Jacobs	$18.95
4710	Collector's Guide to **Children's Books**, 1850 to 1950, Volume I, Jones	$18.95
5153	Collector's Guide to **Chldren's Books**, 1850 to 1950, Volume II, Jones	$19.95
5596	Collector's Guide to **Children's Books**, 1950 to 1975, Volume III, Jones	$19.95
1441	Collector's Guide to **Post Cards**, Wood	$9.95
2081	Guide to Collecting **Cookbooks**, Allen	$14.95
5825	Huxford's **Old Book** Value Guide, 13th Ed.	$19.95
2080	Price Guide to **Cookbooks** & Recipe Leaflets, Dickinson	$9.95
3973	**Sheet Music** Reference & Price Guide, 2nd Ed., Pafik & Guiheen	$19.95
4654	**Victorian Trade Cards**, Historical Reference & Value Guide, Cheadle	$19.95
4733	**Whitman Juvenile Books**, Brown	$17.95

GLASSWARE

5602	Anchor Hocking's **Fire-King** & More, 2nd Ed.	$24.95
4561	Collectible **Drinking Glasses**, Chase & Kelly	$17.95
5823	Collectible **Glass Shoes**, 2nd Edition, Wheatley	$24.95
5357	Coll. **Glassware** from the 40s, 50s & 60s, 5th Ed., Florence	$19.95
1810	Collector's Encyclopedia of **American Art Glass**, Shuman	$29.95
5358	Collector's Encyclopedia of **Depression Glass**, 14th Ed., Florence	$19.95
1961	Collector's Encyclopedia of **Fry Glassware**, Fry Glass Society	$24.95
1664	Collector's Encyclopedia of **Heisey Glass**, 1925–1938, Bredehoft	$24.95
3905	Collector's Encyclopedia of **Milk Glass**, Newbound	$24.95
4936	Collector's Guide to **Candy Containers**, Dezso/Poirier	$19.95
4564	**Crackle Glass**, Weitman	$19.95
4941	**Crackle Glass**, Book II, Weitman	$19.95
4714	**Czechoslovakian Glass** and Collectibles, Book II, Barta/Rose	$16.95
5528	Early American **Pattern Glass**, Metz	$17.95
5682	**Elegant Glassware** of the Depression Era, 9th Ed., Florence	$19.95
5614	Field Guide to **Pattern Glass**, McCain	$17.95
3981	Evers' Standard **Cut Glass** Value Guide	$12.95
4659	**Fenton** Art Glass, 1907–1939, Whitmyer	$24.95
5615	Florence's **Glassware Pattern Identification** Guide, Vol. II	$19.95

4719	**Fostoria**, Etched, Carved & Cut Designs, Vol. II, Kerr	$24.95
3883	**Fostoria Stemware**, The Crystal for America, Long/Seate	$24.95
5261	**Fostoria Tableware**, 1924 – 1943, Long/Seate	$24.95
5361	**Fostoria Tableware**, 1944 – 1986, Long/Seate	$24.95
5604	**Fostoria**, Useful & Ornamental, Long/Seate	$29.95
4644	**Imperial Carnival Glass**, Burns	$18.95
5827	**Kitchen Glassware** of the Depression Years, 6th Ed., Florence	$24.95
5600	Much More Early American **Pattern Glass**, Metz	$17.95
5690	Pocket Guide to **Depression Glass**, 12th Ed., Florence	$9.95
5594	Standard Encyclopedia of **Carnival Glass**, 7th Ed., Edwards/Carwile	$29.95
5595	Standard **Carnival Glass** Price Guide, 12th Ed., Edwards/Carwile	$9.95
5272	Standard Encyclopedia of **Opalescent Glass**, 3rd Ed., Edwards/Carwile	$24.95
5617	Standard Encyclopedia of **Pressed Glass**, 2nd Ed., Edwards/Carwile	$29.95
4731	**Stemware Identification**, Featuring Cordials with Values, Florence	$24.95
4732	**Very Rare Glassware** of the Depression Years, 5th Series, Florence	$24.95
4656	**Westmoreland Glass**, Wilson	$24.95

POTTERY

4927	**ABC Plates & Mugs**, Lindsay	$24.95
4929	**American Art Pottery**, Sigafoose	$24.95
4630	**American Limoges**, Limoges	$24.95
1312	**Blue & White Stoneware**, McNerney	$9.95
1958	So. Potteries **Blue Ridge Dinnerware**, 3rd Ed., Newbound	$14.95
1959	**Blue Willow**, 2nd Ed., Gaston	$14.95
4851	Collectible **Cups & Saucers**, Harran	$18.95
1373	Collector's Encyclopedia of **American Dinnerware**, Cunningham	$24.95
4931	Collector's Encyclopedia of **Bauer Pottery**, Chipman	$24.95
4932	Collector's Encyclopedia of **Blue Ridge Dinnerware**, Vol. II, Newbound	$24.95
4658	Collector's Encyclopedia of **Brush-McCoy Pottery**, Huxford	$24.95
5034	Collector's Encyclopedia of **California Pottery**, 2nd Ed., Chipman	$24.95
2133	Collector's Encyclopedia of **Cookie Jars**, Roerig	$24.95
3723	Collector's Encyclopedia of **Cookie Jars**, Book II, Roerig	$24.95
4939	Collector's Encyclopedia of **Cookie Jars**, Book III, Roerig	$24.95
5748	Collector's Encyclopedia of **Fiesta**, 9th Ed., Huxford	$24.95
4718	Collector's Encyclopedia of **Figural Planters & Vases**, Newbound	$19.95
3961	Collector's Encyclopedia of **Early Noritake**, Alden	$24.95
1439	Collector's Encyclopedia of **Flow Blue China**, Gaston	$19.95
3812	Collector's Encyclopedia of **Flow Blue China**, 2nd Ed., Gaston	$24.95
3431	Collector's Encyclopedia of **Homer Laughlin China**, Jasper	$24.95
1276	Collector's Encyclopedia of **Hull Pottery**, Roberts	$19.95
3962	Collector's Encyclopedia of **Lefton China**, DeLozier	$19.95
4855	Collector's Encyclopedia of **Lefton China**, Book II, DeLozier	$19.95
5609	Collector's Encyclopedia of **Limoges Porcelain**, 3rd Ed., Gaston	$29.95
2334	Collector's Encyclopedia of **Majolica Pottery**, Katz-Marks	$19.95
1358	Collector's Encyclopedia of **McCoy Pottery**, Huxford	$19.95
5677	Collector's Encyclopedia of **Niloak**, 2nd Edition, Gifford	$29.95
3837	Collector's Encyclopedia of **Nippon Porcelain**, Van Patten	$24.95
1665	Collector's Ency. of **Nippon Porcelain**, 3rd Series, Van Patten	$24.95
4712	Collector's Ency. of **Nippon Porcelain**, 4th Series, Van Patten	$24.95
5053	Collector's Ency. of **Nippon Porcelain**, 5th Series, Van Patten	$24.95
5678	Collector's Ency. of **Nippon Porcelain**, 6th Series, Van Patten	$29.95
1447	Collector's Encyclopedia of **Noritake**, Van Patten	$19.95
1038	Collector's Encyclopedia of **Occupied Japan**, 2nd Series, Florence	$14.95
4951	Collector's Encyclopedia of **Old Ivory China**, Hillman	$24.95
5564	Collector's Encyclopedia of **Pickard China**, Reed	$29.95
3877	Collector's Encyclopedia of **R.S. Prussia**, 4th Series, Gaston	$24.95
5679	Collector's Encyclopedia of **Red Wing Art Pottery**, Dollen	$24.95
5618	Collector's Encyclopedia of **Rosemeade Pottery**, Dommel	$24.95
5841	Collector's Encyclopedia of **Roseville Pottery**, Revised, Huxford/Nickel	$24.95
5842	Collector's Encyclopedia of **Roseville Pottery**, 2nd Series, Huxford/Nickel	$24.95
4713	Collector's Encyclopedia of **Salt Glaze Stoneware**, Taylor/Lowrance	$24.95
3314	Collector's Encyclopedia of **Van Briggle Art Pottery**, Sasicki	$24.95
4563	Collector's Encyclopedia of **Wall Pockets**, Newbound	$19.95
2111	Collector's Encyclopedia of **Weller Pottery**, Huxford	$29.95
5680	Collector's Guide to **Feather Edge Ware**, McAllister	$19.95
3876	Collector's Guide to **Lu-Ray Pastels**, Meehan	$18.95

3814	Collector's Guide to **Made in Japan Ceramics**, White	$18.95
4646	Collector's Guide to **Made in Japan Ceramics**, Book II, White	$18.95
2339	Collector's Guide to **Shawnee Pottery**, Vanderbilt	$19.95
1425	**Cookie Jars**, Westfall	$9.95
3440	**Cookie Jars**, Book II, Westfall	$19.95
4924	Figural & Novelty **Salt & Pepper Shakers**, 2nd Series, Davern	$24.95
2379	Lehner's Ency. of **U.S. Marks** on Pottery, Porcelain & China	$24.95
4722	**McCoy Pottery**, Collector's Reference & Value Guide, Hanson/Nissen	$19.95
5691	**Post86 Fiesta**, Identification & Value Guide, Racheter	$19.95
1670	**Red Wing Collectibles**, DePasquale	$9.95
1440	**Red Wing Stoneware**, DePasquale	$9.95
1632	**Salt & Pepper Shakers**, Guarnaccia	$9.95
5091	**Salt & Pepper Shakers** II, Guarnaccia	$18.95
3443	**Salt & Pepper Shakers** IV, Guarnaccia	$18.95
3738	**Shawnee Pottery**, Mangus	$24.95
4629	Turn of the Century **American Dinnerware**, 1880s–1920s, Jasper	$24.95
3327	**Watt Pottery** – Identification & Value Guide, Morris	$19.95

OTHER COLLECTIBLES

5838	Advertising **Thermometers**, Merritt	$16.95
4704	Antique & Collectible **Buttons**, Wisniewski	$19.95
2269	Antique **Brass & Copper** Collectibles, Gaston	$16.95
1880	Antique **Iron**, McNerney	$9.95
3872	Antique **Tins**, Dodge	$24.95
4845	Antique **Typewriters & Office Collectibles**, Rehr	$19.95
5607	Antiquing and Collecting on the **Internet**, Parry	$12.95
1128	**Bottle** Pricing Guide, 3rd Ed., Cleveland	$7.95
3718	Collectible **Aluminum**, Grist	$16.95
4560	Collectible **Cats**, An Identification & Value Guide, Book II, Fyke	$19.95
5060	Collectible **Souvenir Spoons**, Bednersh	$19.95
5676	Collectible **Souvenir Spoons**, Book II, Bednersh	$29.95
5666	Collector's Encyclopedia of **Granite Ware**, Book 2, Greguire	$29.95
5836	Collector's Guide to **Antique Radios**, 5th Ed., Bunis	$19.95
5608	Collector's Gde. to Buying, Selling & Trading on the **Internet**, 2nd Ed., Hix	$12.95
4637	Collector's Guide to **Cigarette Lighters**, Book II, Flanagan	$17.95
3966	Collector's Guide to **Inkwells**, Identification & Values, Badders	$18.95
4947	Collector's Guide to **Inkwells**, Book II, Badders	$19.95
5681	Collector's Guide to **Lunchboxes**, White	$19.95
5621	Collector's Guide to **Online Auctions**, Hix	$12.95
4862	Collector's Guide to **Toasters** & Accessories, Greguire	$19.95
4652	Collector's Guide to **Transistor Radios**, 2nd Ed., Bunis	$16.95
4864	Collector's Guide to **Wallace Nutting Pictures**, Ivankovich	$18.95
1629	**Doorstops**, Identification & Values, Bertoia	$9.95
5683	**Fishing Lure** Collectibles, 2nd Ed., Murphy/Edmisten	$29.95
5259	**Flea Market Trader**, 12th Ed., Huxford	$9.95
4945	**G-Men and FBI Toys** and Collectibles, Whitworth	$18.95
5605	**Garage Sale & Flea Market Annual**, 8th Ed.	$19.95
3819	**General Store** Collectibles, Wilson	$24.95
5159	Huxford's Collectible **Advertising**, 4th Ed.	$24.95
2216	**Kitchen Antiques**, 1790–1940, McNerney	$14.95
5686	**Lighting Fixtures** of the Depression Era, Book I, Thomas	$24.95
4950	The **Lone Ranger**, Collector's Reference & Value Guide, Felbinger	$18.95
2026	**Railroad** Collectibles, 4th Ed., Baker	$14.95
5619	**Roy Rogers and Dale Evans** Toys & Memorabilia, Coyle	$24.95
5692	**Schroeder's Antiques Price Guide**, 19th Ed., Huxford	$14.95
5007	**Silverplated Flatware**, Revised 4th Edition, Hagan	$18.95
5694	Summers' **Guide to Coca-Cola**, 3rd Ed.	$24.95
5356	Summers' **Pocket Guide to Coca-Cola**, 2nd Ed.	$9.95
3892	**Toy & Miniature Sewing Machines**, Thomas	$18.95
4876	**Toy & Miniature Sewing Machines**, Book II, Summers	$24.95
5144	**Value Guide to Advertising Memorabilia**, 2nd Ed., Summers	$19.95
3977	Value Guide to **Gas Station Memorabilia**, Summers & Priddy	$24.95
4877	**Vintage Bar Ware**, Visakay	$24.95
4935	The **W.F. Cody Buffalo Bill** Collector's Guide with Values	$24.95
5281	**Wanted to Buy**, 7th Edition	$9.95

This is only a partial listing of the books on antiques that are available from Collector Books. All books are well illustrated and contain current values. Most of these books are available from your local bookseller, antique dealer, or public library. If you are unable to locate certain titles in your area, you may order by mail from COLLECTOR BOOKS, P.O. Box 3009, Paducah, KY 42002-3009. Customers with Visa, Discover or MasterCard may phone in orders from 7:00–5:00 CST, Monday–Friday, Toll Free 1-800-626-5420, or online at www.collectorbooks.com. Add $3.00 for postage for the first book ordered and 50¢ for each additional book. Include item number, title, and price when ordering. Allow 14 to 21 days for delivery.